HELP! I'M GI

HELP!
I'm Growing Up

ROGER AND CHRISTINE DAY

KINGSWAY PUBLICATIONS
EASTBOURNE

ISBN 0 85476 540 9

Produced by Bookprint Creative Services
P.O. Box 827, BN21 3YJ, England, for
KINGSWAY PUBLICATIONS LTD
Lottbridge Drove, Eastbourne, E Sussex BN23 6NT.
Printed in Great Britain.

To

Simon, Robert and Steven,
three young people who listened, asked questions
and made helpful comments

Contents

Foreword

We live in a record-breaking world. In fact, there are more records being broken today then ever before!

While many are good and worthwhile, some of these records are in fact tragedies of our time.

For instance: there are more abortions than in all of history; the spread of sexual diseases — including AIDS — has reached epidemic proportions in many countries of the world; and larger numbers of marriages end in divorce, often with tragic results for the children.

It's as if people are trying to climb the mountain of life without a map or compass. Many seem to have lost their way in the area of sex and marriage, turning to their own instincts and becoming even more confused as a result.

Young people need to have a reference point as they learn about sex and growing up. That's why I welcome this book. I strongly recommend that parents go through it with their children before they face the pressures of puberty and adolescence.

Then, because this book is based on principles set out in the Bible, young people will be able to use it as a map and compass to guide them through the often difficult teen years.

The longing of my heart is to see a new record broken — by thousands of young people living according to God's standards in our world today.

Roy Castle

Message to young people

Sex is probably the most talked-about, written-about, sung-about and joked-about subject in the world today. Yet many young people are confused with half-truths or downright lies.

If you learn about sex only at school, you may end up not knowing what is right and wrong. If you find out about it just from your friends, they may make things up that for years you'll believe are true.

Reading Together

In this book we're going to tell you as honestly as we can *everything* you need to know about sex — at least until you get married. We recommend that you read it through with one of your parents — Dad if you're a boy, Mum if you're a girl — and talk about the subjects as you go along.

Some of the material may be embarrassing to either you or your parents. Don't be ashamed about blushing. Laugh together, then carry on learning. Sex is a fun subject to find out about in this way. Make the most of it!

You'll see in the various chapters blank spaces to fill in. Most of the answers to these are found in the Bible. Get hold of a modern version (such as the Good News Bible or New International Version), look up the references and write in the answers. You'll be surprised how enjoyable it is.

Future Use

Once you've read the book, we strongly advise you to keep it in a safe place right through your teen years. Use it to look up things as you come across them at school. Refer back to sections that you read when you were too young to understand them fully.

Use the *Contents* to find the main chapters. For example, if you want to read up about homosexuality find the chapter:

Look in the section *Some words and their meaning* for definitions of words that you're not sure about, for example:

> **hymen** — a membrane that partly covers the entrance
> to the vagina of an unmarried girl or woman

Use the *Index* to look up all references to a subject you're interested in. (The darker numbers indicate the most important pages on that subject.) For example:

masturbation 23, 47, 64, **68-72**, 75

Finally, if you want to test yourself on your knowledge of sex, use the section *Some questions about sex.* Try to copy some of the drawings in the early part of this book. Then label the parts without looking back at the originals. It can be geat fun!

(Don't show your drawings to younger brothers and sisters or grandparents without checking with your parents first. Some older people, especially, might be a bit shocked because, when they were young, these things weren't talked about much.)

Like every other young person in the whole world, you're going to face temptations in the area of sex over the next few years. Arm yourself with the truth now and you won't foolishly do things that you'll regret for the rest of your life.

Roger & Christine Day

October 1986

Message to parents

People who give their pre-teen child a book on sex and then feel they have 'done their duty' are opting out of one of their most important God-given responsibilities as parents. That's why this book is intended to be read by young people *with* their parents.

If we're honest, though, we have to admit that talking about some aspects of sex — even in this so-called liberated age — can be acutely embarrassing.

Not so long ago, a board game was invented in California as a 'tool for helping parents who have difficulty discussing sex with their children'. The board itself had pictures of male and female genitals and the baby's development in the womb. It was played using an egg token which was pursued by three sperm tokens along a twisting course representing the Fallopian tube.

The idea was that this just *might* help parents to open up a conversation with their children!

Why So Detailed?

We have tried to be a bit more straightforward in this book. In fact, you won't have to read very far before you realise that we have covered subjects in here which were taboo ten years ago or even less, particularly among some Christians.

So why, in a sex education book primarily for prepubic children, is it necessary to be so detailed? The answer, quite simply, is that your children will soon be (or may already have been) confronted with the most incredible details about sex, much of it perverted and confusing. They will also be put under intense pressure from their peers to indulge in sexual activity of all sorts.

Misguided teachers may instil into them some of the lies of the so-called 'liberated age' about sex before marriage, homosexuality, incest, bestiality and other wrong aspects of sex.

Knowing what to expect and what the Christian and biblical attitude should be are, we believe, two of the steps towards winning that battle.

The School's Task?

Some well-meaning parents have in the past been quite willing to leave the embarrassing details of sex education to the school classroom. After all, they've argued, it might not be moral teaching — but at least it's not immoral.

Sadly, unless your child is in a school staffed entirely by people upholding biblical truths, this is something that can no longer be assumed.

A few years ago a source list of school teaching books on sex prepared by the British government-financed Health Education Council included publications which gave support to homosexual, lesbian and bisexual relationships; explored sexual alternatives to marriage; detailed dozens of sexual positions; discussed loss of virginity; and explained the range of contraceptives available to teenagers.

And that's after the list was heavily pruned by government ministers following national publicity given to the highly objectionable material previously included!

In June 1986 the British Government announced plans to change sex education in state schools with the aim of 'encouraging pupils to have due regard to moral considerations and the value of family life'. Responsibility for effecting the change was put on local education authorities, governors and head teachers.

It has a long way to go before such ideals can be achieved. The 1986 syllabus for certain examinations in biology (intended for children aged about 14 to 16) included details of sex without pregnancy, masturbation, homosexual practices and abortion!

Propaganda

Even more serious is the way sex education is used in some schools to put across immoral propaganda. The Association of Christian Teachers said in October 1986: 'There is much responsible, wholesome sex education going on in schools . . . . The good work is jeopardised by fanatics who believe that the most interesting thing about a person is his orientation, and that sexual self-satisfaction is a supreme and sacred right.'

Perhaps the strongest lobby is from the homosexual community. Among books in some London school libraries was one depicting a five-year-old girl in bed with her father and his homosexual lover. It provoked strong reaction from government ministers who, in an unprecedented move, appealed for it to be withdrawn.

The Campaign for Homosexual Equality wants children to be taught that it is perfectly normal to be 'gay'. In a controversial leaflet it wrote: 'Lesbian and gay school students should be free to be open about their sexuality and to discuss it without fear of reproof or violence.'

Homosexual militants are also active in the teaching unions, according to Rachel Tingle, an economist and journalist. She pointed out in a leaflet that motions to union conferences had included calls for 'gay' teachers to support paedophiles — adults who engage in sex with children.

A Positive Approach

Of course, not all teachers are instructing children in sexual promiscuity. Far from it! The majority are dedicated, caring people whose priority is to train children to be decent responsible adults. It's just that, so often, the minority of teachers advocating such wrong views seem to have a louder voice.

There are many groups and organisations seeking to encourage a positive, biblical approach to sex education in schools. They include the Association of Christian Teachers and CARE Trust, together with its sister group, CARE Campaigns, which lobbies for changes to the law in order to uphold moral standards in Britain.

Unhelpful Books

While we were researching for this book, we looked at a wide range of the books on sex education currently available. Most have their good points but some we see as being positively harmful. Our local library supplied us with two well-known ones — their entire stock of such books.

One of these is intended to be given to children aged 12 and over and contains many explicit life-like drawings. It advocates masturbation as 'a kind of practice for adult sex' but also an enjoyable act to be used throughout life; suggests that teenagers going out together 'give each other a climax with their hands'; takes a neutral line on homosexuality; and says that there is nothing wrong with pornography, which enables boys and grown men 'to imagine sexual things which would please or excite them and make masturbation more fun'.

The other book is aimed at 9s to 12s. There is a strong emphasis on nudity for its own sake, with several unnecessary photographs. The book is totally neutral on moral standards; says nothing about marriage or parental responsibility; and encourages early sterilisation of a woman as a form of contraception.

Acceptable Alternative

There are, no doubt, some good, wholesome books still around. But they've become the exception rather than the rule.

This book, we hope, will be much more acceptable in the majority of families than many of these alternatives. It has been divided into bite-sized chapters that the father and son or mother and daughter can go through together over a number of days or weeks.

If your child is particularly young (up to, say, about nine or ten), you may want to go through the first half of the book and leave the remainder for a year or two.

Why a Biblical Basis?

The material in this book is unashamedly based on the Bible. Some may wonder why this is so.

A few years ago restoration work started on the outside of a 900-year-old church building in the Soviet Union. Two years later, when the scaffolding was removed, the building collapsed in a crumbling heap of worthless masonry!

Many well-meaning teachers and parents today are starting from the assumption that children will inevitably be promiscuous. By providing information about contraception, abortion and 'safe sex', they are merely patching up the outside of the building.

A child's sexual identity, as well as his education in these matters, must be built on firm foundations with solidly-built walls. The Bible provides those foundations. Build on that, adapting the material in this book to suit your own family situation and attitudes, and there is less likelihood of a crumbling heap when your child hits the sexual battles of the teen years.

Because this book is based on Christian principles, we have provided relevant Bible references to look up together. The child then fills in blank spaces based on those references.

This doesn't mean, however, that it is intended to be restricted to committed Christians. The very fact that the Bible has so much to say on the subject of sex only serves to demonstrate how comprehensive and relevant it is to everyone in today's world.

A Source Book

Each child is different. Some may feel overwhelmed at the prospect of writing the answers in this book. If that is the case, or you don't have access to a Bible, please don't feel under any obligation to follow these suggestions.

At the end of each chapter there is a discussion idea. This is an opportunity for the parent to make sure that the child has grasped the subject as far as he is able. It is also a chance for you both to talk openly about the temptations your child will face in the future.

Later, when he is going through those same difficulties, your child may be too embarrassed to talk openly. Rereading parts of this book may be his only recourse — so make sure he doesn't throw it away or lose it!

At the end of the book there are a number of questions which your child might like to try as a written quiz, either now or in the future. Suggest it to him as a kind of fun exercise, not a chore that *must* be done.

If you want to use this book with more than one child, we strongly advise you to invest in a copy for each of them. It is, as we've said, intended as a reference book to be used throughout the teen years, and no doubt the child would prefer to keep his own copy handy without having to ask you for it every time he has a question!

Once you have gone through it with your child, we strongly recommend that you give him a copy of James Dobson's *Preparing for Adolescence* (Kingsway), which covers the emotional battles he will face as a teenager. Roger's first book, *How to Grow Up as a Christian Boy or Girl* (New Frontiers), might also prove helpful.

It's possible that you will disagree with some of the views expressed in this book. If so, don't be afraid to make your position clear to your child.

You may also be tempted to protect your child from some of the explicit information contained in the book. One thing is certain, though. However controversial some of these subjects are, they *will* be discussed by children in the school playground. Far better to hear them from you than to receive half truths from their friends.

What About Single Parents?

If you are a single parent, particularly if your child is the opposite sex to you, you may want to consider asking a man to teach your son or a woman to teach your daughter. We would recommend this, though there are no hard and fast rules about it.

How do you go about finding such a person? First, the person needs to be married, preferably with children of his own. Second, he should know your child reasonably well or be able to spend time befriending your child before going through this book and talking about sex.

Third, once you've decided on the person (such as a youth group leader, or a church leader or his wife), discuss with him as frankly as you are able the approach he will be taking and his stance on moral issues that particularly concern you.

Have Fun!

One final suggestion: Don't suddenly become serious when you explore sex education together. As you go through this book, try to make it fun for both you and your child.

Have a good laugh, by all means. Far more important than your *knowledge* of sex is your *attitude* to it. God wants your child to enjoy sex when he grows up. Help him to look forward to it, not fear it.

May you have the wisdom of Solomon, the patience of Job and the joy of the Lord as you take your child through these truths.

Roger & Christine Day
October 1986

1

Why sex?

Have you ever wondered why there are more jokes about sex than any other subject?

The main reason is that most people find it difficult or embarrassing to talk about something so important and they think it's easier to laugh about it. How wrong they are!

In this book we hope to tell you in a straight, simple, honest way why God gave us sex, what it's all about and how you, as a young person, can live a pure life in an impure world. But we hope you'll also enjoy reading these chapters — and even be able to smile now and again.

First of all, why sex? After all, God must have known that people would use sex wrongly.

The answer is that God has two main reasons for making us sexual beings: reproduction and enjoyment.

Reproduction

Reproduction simply means having a part in producing a new life. In Genesis 1 verse 28, God told the first man and woman, 'Have many children, so that your descendants will live all over the earth and bring it under their control.'

People have been very good at that over the years. Today there are about five billion people in the world to prove it. At least Adam and Eve, as well as people since, didn't make a mistake there.

Animals also reproduce. Usually this, too, is sexual reproduction. In other words, a male and female cell join together and then grow into a new creature.

Sexual reproduction in animals makes sure that the new life produced has some things similar to both its mother and father. But it's slightly different from every other animal.

Some simple animals have a cell that just splits off a new life without sexual joining. The animals produced in this way tend to be all the same. Wouldn't it be boring if people all looked alike?

God knew what he was doing when he invented sex.

Enjoyment

Sex is also something that is very enjoyable. A married man and woman have their closest moments in bed together, enjoying each other's body.

In the past, some people who haven't understood God's goodness to them have got married and then thought they had to wait until they wanted children before they had sex together.

How silly! The Bible clearly teaches that a husband and wife should *enjoy* sex together. In 1 Corinthians 7 verses 2 to 5 we read about the husband and wife giving their bodies to each other sexually. (If you want to know more about God's attitude to sex, read Song of Songs [Solomon] 2 verses 3 to 17 and 4 verses 1 to 7; Proverbs 5 verses 18 to 19.)

Animals, on the other hand, don't have the same kind of sexual enjoyment as people. For them, sex is only for reproduction.

Because sex is such an enjoyable gift and sexual temptations can be so strong, many young people believe the lies they hear all around them and try to enjoy sex before they get married. This usually results in misery instead of enjoyment, as we'll see in a later chapter.

With so much wrong sex around, some people think of *all* sex as being wrong or dirty or evil. Write down what God says about that (first part of Hebrews 13 verse 4).

_____

_____

_____

_____

_____

_____   (See also Proverbs 5 verse 19.)

Sex is *not* wrong. It only becomes wrong when it takes place between two people who aren't married.

Growing Up

One day your body will begin growing up sexually, if it hasn't done so already. Then you'll start facing much stronger sexual temptations. You will often wonder how you can possibly manage without sex for ten or even 20 years until you're married.

We hope that, as a result of this book and with the help of your parents, you'll be able to live a life free from sexual sin and eagerly look forward to enjoying sex and all the other good things of married life.

Something to talk about

It says in 1 Timothy 6 verse 17 that God gave us everything for our

_____

Does that include sex? Why?

2

Know yourself

At your age you probably know quite a bit about your body and how it works.

In this chapter we thought it would be a good idea to describe the sex organs (*genitals*) of a boy and a girl, as well as showing you what the different parts look like. As you know, there are many names for the various parts. But we'll be using the proper names right through this book so it's important to find out exactly what we're talking about.

A Boy's Body

Most of a boy's sex organs are easy to see. They consist of his penis — a fleshy tube-like organ — and two testicles that hang in their own special bag of skin (the scrotum) under the penis. We'll mention the hidden parts as we go along.

The *penis* is the main sex organ. It consists of a *shaft* and a very sensitive head part known as the *glans*. All boys are born with a flap of skin covering this head. It is called the *prepuce* (or *foreskin*) and is sometimes cut away by a small operation called *circumcision*.

Running through the centre of the penis is a tube called the *urethra*. Usually this carries the urine away from the *bladder* when the boy goes to the toilet. But later, the same tube will be used for sperm to pass out of the body during sex and at other times. A special valve makes sure that urine and sperm never pass through at the same time.

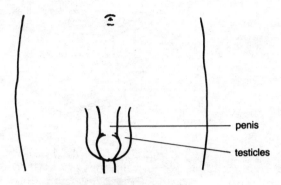

A boy's sex organs

(front view)

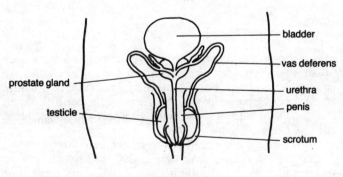

(inside view)

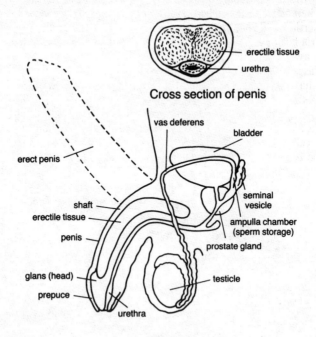

erectile tissue

urethra

Cross section of penis

vas deferens

bladder

erect penis

seminal vesicle

shaft

erectile tissue

penis

ampulla chamber (sperm storage)

prostate gland

glans (head)

prepuce

testicle

urethra

A boy's sex organs
(side view)

The penis has an amazing ability to go hard and stiff, becoming much larger than it was before and sticking up on average at an angle of 45°. This is called an *erection* and is caused by blood rushing into three columns of special, sponge-like *erectile tissue* in the penis. It's a bit like filling a balloon with water — before, it is soft and floppy; after, it is stiff and keeps its shape.

Sex would be impossible without an erection because the soft penis would never go into the woman's vagina. But, as every boy knows, erections can happen at a lot of other times, too, sometimes for no apparent reason.

Just below the penis is the *scrotum* containing two *testicles,* one of which is usually slightly lower than the other. The scrotum controls the temperature of the testicles by shrinking and expanding closer to or further away from the body.

When a boy has been swimming in the cold sea, he will notice that the scrotum shrinks and holds the testicles tightly against his body. After a hot bath, though, the scrotum expands and the testicles hang a bit away from the body.

This is because, when sperm cells start being produced in the testicles, they have to be kept at a slightly lower temperature than the rest of the body.

When the testicles start working at puberty (the stage where a boy begins to get his adult body), they produce up to 500 million tiny *sperm cells* a day. These are carried through the sperm duct *(vas deferens)* to the *ampulla* (or *storage chamber),* where they are stored.

During sex, after the boy is married, the sperm is mixed to form a sticky, white cloudy liquid called *semen* and about a teaspoonful of this spurts out of the end of the erect penis into the woman's vagina. (This happens with the help of the *seminal vesicle, ejaculatory duct, prostate gland* and *Cowper's gland.*)

After puberty and before marriage, semen is removed in the same way every few days or weeks when the storage chamber fills up with sperm. While he's asleep, the boy's penis will become erect and semen will spurt out into his pyjamas. This is called a *nocturnal emission* and is perfectly normal and natural. It is often called a *wet dream* because it can be accompanied by a dream about sex — though a dream isn't necessary for a nocturnal emmission to occur.

Semen also spurts out of the penis if a boy masturbates (plays with himself sexually). We'll talk about that in a later chapter.

A Girl's Body

A girl's sex organs are more difficult to see than those of a boy. The slit-like opening between a girl's legs is called the *vulva* area. It consists of a fleshy part *(mons pubis),* an outer and inner set of *lips* (or *labia)* and the opening to the *vagina,* the main sex organ. There is also the *urethra* opening, used only for carrying urine from the *bladder.*

Buried under the skin of the vulva area is a small organ called the *clitoris.* This is very sensitive and its purpose is to help with sexual enjoyment. It can become hard and erect at any time — especially during sexual excitement — but, of course, doesn't stick up like the penis. Only its end can be seen.

The vagina is designed to receive the penis during sex but its moist, elastic walls can open up to 10 cm (4 inches) or more in diameter when a baby passes through it at birth.

In girls who have never had sex, the opening to the vagina is usually partly covered by a membrane called the *hymen,* though this might occasionally stretch open during sport or horseriding.

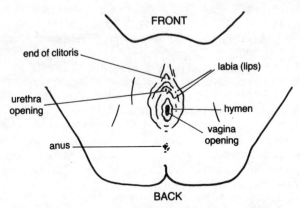

A girl's sex organs from underneath
(with legs apart)

When a married woman first has sex, she usually finds that this stretches or tears open fully. Occasionally, if the hymen is particularly tough, the stretching may have to be done by a doctor before marriage.

The vagina leads into the *cervix* or neck of the *uterus (womb).* The uterus is the size and shape of a small pear but its thick walls can expand by an amazing amount when the baby grows in it during pregnancy.

Leading into the top of the uterus are two *Fallopian tubes,* which act like funnels, catching and carrying the tiny eggs from the two almond-sized *ovaries* to the uterus. It is in these tubes that, if sex has taken place, *fertilisation* occurs. In other words, the egg (from the wife) and sperm (from the husband) join together to form an *embryo* which then has a chance to grow and become a baby.

At the same time, the uterus forms a special lining with a lot of blood vessels in it (the *placenta)* to receive the new life. The fertilised egg then fixes on to this lining and the baby starts to develop.

An *egg* (or *ovum)* smaller than a pinhead is formed about every month after the girl reaches puberty and she becomes sexually mature. Usually, each ovary produces an egg every other month. If it is not fertilised, the egg passes into the uterus and is dissolved.

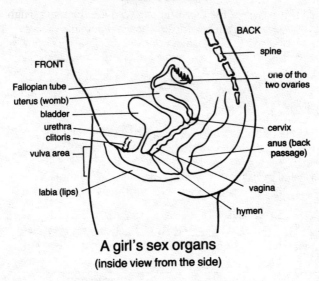

A girl's sex organs
(inside view from the side)

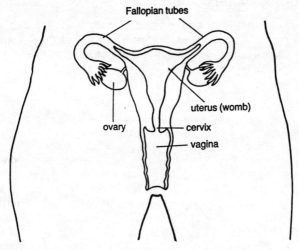

A girl's sex organs
(inside view from the front)

When this happens, the uterus lining, which has built up ready for the fertilised embryo, isn't needed. It breaks up and for the next few days the blood passes out through the vagina. This is called a *period* and during it the girl will wear some kind of pad to absorb the blood.

Good or Bad?

Some people think that parts of their body are good while others are somehow bad or dirty or sinful. Don't ever allow yourself to think like that.

God made every part of your body, including the sexual parts. In what way did he arrange them (1 Corinthians 12 verse 18)?

_____

When God finished creating the world, including people with their sex organs, what did he think of it all (Genesis 1 verse 31)?

_____

We hope you'll learn to be grateful for the way *you've* been made.

Something to talk about

See if you can remember where you'd find the following and what they're for: uterus, testicles, vagina, penis, Fallopian tube, scrotum, ovary, erectile tissue. If you're not sure about some of them, reread this chapter, study the drawings and try again.

3

The joy of marriage

You don't have to read much of the second part of the Bible (the New Testament) before you realise that there is a lot in it about love. Spend a few minutes reading 1 Corinthians 13 and you'll see what we mean.

God speaks about love between a man and a woman as something very, very special. Husbands are told to love their wives in the same

way as _____

_____

(Ephesians 5 verse 25). Or, as it says in verses 28 to 29, they should

love their wives _____

_____ .

Wives, of course, are also taught to love their husbands (Titus 2 verses 4 to 5).

But what *is* love? If you listened only to what pop songs say, you would think love meant just sex. But love is much, much more than that.

Love is devoted attachment, affection, kindness, fondness, admiration, caring, sharing and tenderness. That's why a husband and wife like to spend lots of time together, just learning how to love each other more and more. And the deepest expression of that love is in the act of sex.

Sexual Love

Sex in marriage is something that a loving couple don't rush. They might first just spend time together, enjoying one another's company and talking about how much they love each other.

Often sex comes naturally out of that. The husband and wife will undress and get into bed together, though occasionally they might enjoy sex somewhere else. They begin with a lot of kissing and cuddling, which becomes more exciting as it goes along.

Gradually they also start touching each other's body in various ways and places, particularly the sex organs and the wife's breasts. (This is known as *foreplay.)*

All this helps them both to get ready for the actual sex act.

When they are fully ready, the wife opens her legs and the husband carefully and gently slips his penis into her vagina. This is possible because the penis by this time is erect and very stiff and the vagina has enlarged slightly and become moist and slippery.

A husband and wife enjoying the sex act

Then they both begin to move. At first the movements might be just wriggling around. Gradually, though, the movement becomes faster and faster, more and more exciting, as the husband moves his penis up and down inside the vagina and the woman moves in response. Suddenly the sperm comes out of the end of the penis into the vagina in a series of powerful squirts.

This is called an *ejaculation* (or *climax).* The wife quite often also reaches a climax (or *orgasm),* though of course nothing is squirted out (ejaculated) as is the case with the man.

A Happy Ending

The climax is the most enjoyable part of the sex act. For the man it's like a series of enjoyable explosions, while the climax in the woman is like pleasant waves washing over her. In both cases the whole body is involved and it's an experience to look forward to and to remember happily afterwards.

All this takes as long as half an hour or more in bed and is something very, very pleasant for both of them. It's also relaxing and they will often fall into a happy sleep in each other's arms!

Men usually reach a climax easily, but the climax in a woman takes a lot longer. A loving husband learns through patience, care and understanding how to bring his wife to her climax, preferably every time they have sex.

You may have heard of one or two of the problems that married people have during sex. *Frigidity* in a wife means that she isn't interested in sex, is unable to enjoy it properly and can't reach an orgasm.

Husbands have two main problems. The commonest is *premature ejaculation,* when he ejaculates before his wife is fully ready, sometimes even before his penis is inserted into her vagina. The other problem is *impotence,* which means that his penis doesn't become erect at all or goes floppy after a short time. This can be caused by anything from tiredness and feeling ill to fear, worry, drinking too much alcohol or taking drugs.

These problems can be overcome by a husband and wife who learn to care for and understand each other.

Fertilisation

After sex, if a sperm cell meets an egg, fertilisation usually takes place and a baby starts to develop.

Of course, most married couples don't want to have a child every year for the next 20 or 25 years until the wife reaches an age (the *menopause*) when her body no longer produces eggs, her periods stop as a result and she is unable to have a baby. (As with puberty, the exact age at which this happens varies from woman to woman.)

So the married couple take precautions in order to be able to enjoy sex without having babies too often. This is called *contraception.*

Contraception

This takes many forms. The *natural* (or *rhythm)* methods mean that the couple can have sex only on certain days of the month. The wife has to look at charts or check her body temperature to discover the days when she is least likely to get *pregnant.* This is all very complicated and doesn't always work but some people think such methods are a good idea.

The best-known contraceptives are the *Pill,* which a woman takes each day, and the *sheath* (or *condom),* a kind of sausage-shaped balloon that the man stretches over his erect penis to catch the semen. Some women have a *diaphragm (cap)* or a *coil* (also called an *IUD)* placed inside them or they put special *spermicidal foam* into their vagina as a form of contraceptive.

There are also permanent ways of stopping babies. They involve an operation, on either the man or the woman, known as *vasectomy* in the man and *sterilisation* in the woman. People usually think very carefully before agreeing to this, not because it is wrong but because, once done, it is almost impossible to reverse.

All married couples have to face the fact that any kind of contraception, even vasectomy and sterilisation, can go wrong. As a result, the woman might become pregnant when she least expects it.

A husband and wife who find that this has happened may be shocked at first. But almost always they will end up being delighted about their surprise child.

You see, the Bible teaches clearly that there are no unwanted children. God knew about each one of us even before we were born (Psalm 139 verse 13 and the first part of Jeremiah 1 verse 5).

According to Psalm 127 verse 3, children are _____

_____

The child born by 'accident' in marriage is no accident to God.

Young and Old!

You might think that sex is just for young adults who are strong and healthy. Well, you're wrong! Some young people are shocked when they realise for the first time that their parents enjoy sex with each other regularly.

Even more surprising, perhaps, is to know that people as old as your grandparents — or even great grandparents — are often sexually active with their husbands or wives.

If their marriage partners are now dead, they may well be experiencing serious sexual temptations. Those temptations will almost certainly not be as strong at their age as for you when you are in your teen years (see chapter 12). But don't think that getting older means that you don't need to control your body's desires anymore!

Just as surprising is that married people who are disabled, including many of those without arms or legs, usually seem to manage somehow to enjoy sex with each other! It shows what a very, very strong desire for sex God has put in each of us.

An old man with serious heart disease once went to see his doctor.

'I'm sorry,' said the doctor, 'but you're going to have to give up all strenuous activity. That includes sex with your wife. Do it and it'll kill you.'

The old man looked up with a twinkle in his eye and a smile on his face. 'What a way to die!' he exclaimed in delight.

Something to talk about

Some people believe that sex is something just for having children and should not be used for enjoyment. How would you explain God's attitude to this?

4

The price of sexual freedom

In the last chapter we talked about sex in its right place — marriage. It's very enjoyable, something to look forward to and well worth the long wait!

But all around us people are being fooled into trying to enjoy sex wrongly, without realising the price they will have to pay. The main area where this is happening is in having sex before marriage. In this chapter we want to warn you about the price of sexual 'freedom' before you find yourself caught by it.

Bible Reasons

First, what does God have to say about sex outside marriage? Quite simply, he calls it sin. The main kinds are *fornication* (or being *immoral)* and *adultery* (see Ephesians 5 verse 5 and Exodus 20 verse 14). A homosexual act is another kind of sexual sin but we'll deal with that in a separate chapter.

Fornication means having sex without getting married. Many people have foolishly believed that there's nothing really wrong with that.

Adultery is when a married man or woman has sex with someone he or she isn't married to. Millions of marriages around the world have been wrecked by adultery.

As you can see from these verses, God says that *all* sex outside marriage is wrong. In fact, he puts sexual sin in a special class of its own because of the damage it does.

Read 1 Corinthians 6 verses 18 to 20 and write down what sexual

sin is against (verse 18). _____

Why is this important (verse 19)? _____

_____

How should we use our bodies (verse 20)? _____

_____

Commonsense Reasons

It's all very well to tell you not to have sex before marriage because God says you shouldn't. But that may not seem to be a good enough argument when many of your friends start having sex and putting pressure on you to say why you don't. So let's have a look at some other reasons.

Sex outside marriage, like other sins, seems pleasant at the time. But the enjoyment isn't lasting and there's *always* a very high price to pay.

It's a bit like being invited to a really nice free meal with the loveliest food you've ever tasted. Then, after you've tried a mouthful, you realise with horror that it wasn't free after all. In fact, it was so expensive that you'll still be paying for it years from now!

Let's look at the cost of sex for a teenage boy and girl still at school. We'll call them Simon and Tracy.

They've been spending a lot of time together and, because they feel sexually attracted to each other (most boys and girls in their young teens find each other attractive), they think they must be in love. Simon suggests to Tracy that they try out their 'love' by having sex.

Finding somewhere alone is the first problem. When they do, they have to rush things in case they get caught. It's all over in a couple of minutes.

It wasn't as much fun as they expected. In fact, they were both very disappointed. But at least they can now boast about their sexual 'experience'.

Pregnancy

Sadly, that's about all they can boast about. If they are like half the people who first have sex under the age of 16, they won't have used a contraceptive. Tracy could well be pregnant and she will then be forced to decide whether to have an abortion or to become an unmarried mother.

In *abortion,* the developing baby is actually killed (most Christians, and many other people, would say 'murdered'). Girls — and women — who have an abortion often feel guilty and depressed about it for years afterwards.

If she has the baby, at least she won't have the same guilt. But people will know about her sin and, also, her baby will start off in life with many disadvantages.

If she can't bring the baby up herself, there are thousands of married couples who would be happy to adopt her baby and give him a good home. But she may feel guilty that she has had a child and then given him away.

Another possibility is to get married to the person who made her pregnant. More often than not this kind of marriage ends in disaster.

Each of these alternatives has big problems which aren't usually solved easily. How much better to stay free from sexual sin in the first place!

Diseases

But the problems don't stop there. If Simon or Tracy had secretly had sex with someone else before, they could give each other one of the *sexually transmitted diseases* (known simply as STD). These are still sometimes known as venereal diseases (VD). More and more young people are catching them. Many experts describe their spread as an epidemic.

We thought you ought to know a bit about what these diseases are like. Many of them result in very sore areas or warts around the sexual organs. In the case of boys, they can result in a painful burning sensation when urine is passed. Even more common in girls is a thick smelly or itchy liquid that comes out of the vagina. (A small amount of this liquid is quite normal for women and older girls, but it is usually clear, rarely smelly and not really noticeable.)

Unless a person with STD is treated by a doctor or special clinic, the disease can become much worse and lead to other, much more serious, problems. If treated, STD infections, such as *gonorrhoea* and the less common *syphilis,* usually disappear.

But once a person catches *genital herpes* (sometimes called the 'love bug'), which is increasing at a rapid rate, he will probably keep getting it again and again. This very painful disease results in small 'cold sores' appearing around the sex organs. Scientists hope to find a cure in a few years' time, but until then millions of people will be suffering in their bodies because of their sin.

Perhaps the worst disease Tracy could eventually develop because of having sex in her young teens is *cancer of the cervix.* This is spreading at the same rate as sex before marriage and is especially common among women in their 20s who were sexually active as young teenagers.

Women are often checked for this cancer every few years using a

Getting It Wrong

routine test known as a cervical smear. If it is found in time. it can be treated. If not, sadly, there is little that doctors can do.

In a later chapter we'll be talking about another sexual disease called *AIDS*. This affects the body's ability to fight disease.

Up until fairly recently it affected mainly people who committed homosexual sin as well as drug addicts and people who, for medical reasons, had to be injected with large amounts of blood products regularly. Now, more and more, it can also be caught by other boys and girls, men and women, who have sex outside of marriage.

Again, although doctors are trying to find a way of curing AIDS, it almost always leads to death.

Guilt

But disease isn't the only thing Simon and Tracy could suffer from. For many years they are likely to feel guilty about their sin.

When they eventually get married (almost certainly not to each other), those feelings might not go away because their bodies will in one sense be 'secondhand'.

The special God-given joy of discovering sex with partners who are *virgins* (in other words, who have not yet had sex) and with whom they will spend their lives will have gone. And this could seriously affect their marriages.

Saying No

How much better it would have been if Simon and Tracy had resisted the temptation in the first place! Saying 'no' isn't weakness; it takes real strength. Look up and read Titus 2 verses 11 to 14. It says there that the grace of God 'teaches us to say "No" to ungodliness and worldly passions'. (See also 2 Timothy 2 verse 22.)

In Proverbs 7 verses 6 to 27 the brilliant King Solomon tells a story about a weak, silly young man who gets caught in the sex trap. Read about him and then from the last three verses write down in your own words Solomon's advice for avoiding sexual sin. _____

_____

_____

Any young man or woman can get caught in the same sort of trap when it comes to sex. Make sure you don't.

'But I've failed'

It's just possible that you might already have fallen into the sex trap. As a result of reading this, or finding out the results of sexual sin for yourself, you may now feel very guilty about what you've done.

Is there any hope for you?

The answer is, *'Yes!'* Here are the steps you will need to take:

1. Realise that all sin is very wrong. 'God wants you to be . . . completely free from sexual immorality' (1 Thessalonians 4 verse 3). By having sex outside of marriage you have sinned and gone against God's plan for your life.

2. Repent of your sin. 'Repent' means a total change of mind and attitude. It's not just something emotional, or merely 'turning over a new leaf', but involves a determination on your part never to sin again. 'If we confess our sins to God, he will . . . forgive us our sins and purify us from all our wrongdoing' (1 John 1 verse 9).

Then you'll know that you are forgiven (Psalm 103 verse 3) and that God will never again remember your sin (Hebrew 8 verse 12).

3. Receive Jesus Christ as the Lord (or Boss) of your life. 'Some . . . did receive him and believed in him; so he gave them the right to become God's children' (John 1 verse 12). Jesus died to take away your sin (Romans 5 verses 8 to 10) and came back to life again to give you new life (John 10 verse 10). Then join with others in a church where people believe that the Bible is God's Word to people today.

4. Recognise that temptation isn't wrong, but sin is. God has given you those sexual desires — and he wants you to keep them under control until you are married. Remember that every other unmarried person has the same struggle. The secret is to know the power of the Holy Spirit in your life as a day-to-day reality. 'Let the Spirit direct your lives, and you will not satisfy the desires of the human nature' (Galatians 5 verse 16).

5. Retrain your thinking and way of life. Cut off any relationships where sex is involved. Don't mix with others who brag all the time about how many people they have had sex with. Take up your time and energy with something good and positive — join the local football club or take up cycling. Anything will do as long as you can put your effort into it.

For the next few months it's important that you mix in groups until your old way of thinking about sex has been retrained by God. When you do start going out with someone again, decide at the very beginning that you will break off the relationship if things start getting out of hand.

Something to talk about

Imagine that a 14-year-old boy you know says that has decided to have sex with his girlfriend. What sort of things would you say to try to stop him?

5

A new life begins

Your sex education wouldn't be complete if we didn't say something about the exciting way a baby develops in his mother's uterus (womb).

In this chapter we'll describe this very briefly. But we strongly recommend that you also read a larger book on the subject.

As a family, we use *The Complete Book of Baby Care* (Octopus Books), but any book with large, colourful, easy-to-follow pictures would do.

Borrow one out of the library if you need to. It's a fun subject to talk about as a family. And younger brothers and sisters will almost certainly find it fascinating.

A Start in Life

As we said earlier in this book, fertilisation takes place in the Fallopian tube when a male sperm cell joins with the female egg. This doesn't happen every time a couple have sex, even when they're not using contraception. Sometimes a wife might have to wait several months before she becomes pregnant. At other times it happens straightaway.

Of the millions of sperm cells that enter the vagina after sex, a few hundred manage to make their way to the Fallopian tube. But only one pierces through the outer coat of the egg. Immediately that happens, the outer coat becomes like armour plating so that no more can get in.

After about seven or eight days the fertilised egg passes from the Fallopian tube and becomes attached to the lining of the uterus.

The mother's body then starts to produce a blood-rich *placenta* so that the developing embryo (or *foetus*) can be fed. The placenta is connected to the baby's tummy region by the *umbilical cord.*

Christians sometimes disagree about when life actually begins. Some say it's at fertilisation while others think it's when the fertilised embryo fixes on to the uterus.

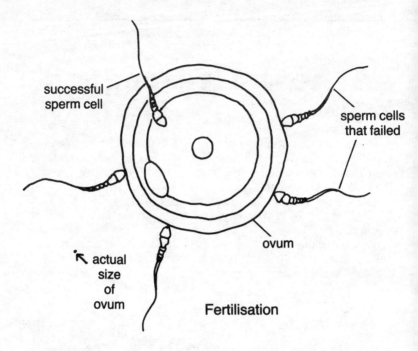

successful
sperm cell

sperm cells
that failed

ovum

↖ actual
size
of
ovum

Fertilisation

But all are agreed on one thing — it's God who gives life to the baby well before birth. And that's something no person — not even a doctor — can fully understand.

Look up Ecclesiastes 11 verse 5 and write it down in your own

words. _____

_____

_____

_____

Eight Weeks

By the time he (or she) is eight weeks old, the foetus is beginning to look like a tiny baby. He is about 2.5cm (1 inch) long and weighs about

2 grammes.

He is attached to the placenta by the umbilical cord and receives all his nourishment through it. He is surrounded and protected by a watery liquid called *amniotic fluid*. His heart is pumping blood around his tiny body, carrying oxygen and food from his mother.

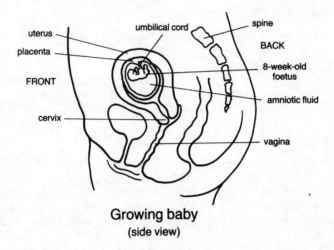

Growing baby
(side view)

At eight weeks, the foetus has arms and legs. Fingers and toes are starting to appear. There are ear, nose and mouth openings and the eyes have developed but are covered by the eyelids.

Twelve Weeks

Four weeks later the foetus weighs about 14 grammes. Fingers and toes are fully formed and the baby is moving regularly. His (or her) sex organs have developed.

In fact, by this age all the baby's major parts are formed. Occasionally something is missing. But the miracle is that almost all babies — with millions of complicated parts — have nothing wrong with them.

King David said in Psalm 139 verses 13 to 16 that God knew us

so well because he _____

_____ .

Twenty Weeks

By 20 weeks the unborn baby's body is covered by thin hair, though the eyes are still closed. The baby now weighs about 300 grammes (8 ounces) and measures 16cm (6.5 inches) from head to bottom.

Thirty Weeks

At this stage the baby is very wrinkled and red. His skin is covered by a white soapy substance (*vernix*) to stop waterlogging. He is usually very active and the mother can feel lots of kicking and moving about. He weighs a bit more than a bag of sugar (a kilo — 2.2 pounds) and is about 25cm (10 inches) from top to bottom.

Forty Weeks

After 40 weeks (nine months) in the uterus, the baby is ready to be born. At this stage he weighs anything from 2 to 4 kilos (4.5 to 9 pounds). He fills the uterus, which has stretched a very long way. He can't move quite as much because of lack of space and is usually upside down with his head at the entrance to the vagina ready for the miracle of birth.

If he's the other way up (bottom nearest to the vagina entrance), he is in what's called the *breech* position. He may then have to have a bit of extra help from the doctors and nurses at birth.

Birth

Birth begins when the muscles of the uterus start to expand and contract regularly, squeezing the baby through the cervix opening. These are called *contractions* and, when they start to become regular, or the fluid surrounding the baby is passed out ('the breaking of the waters'), the mother goes into hospital or prepares to have her baby at home. *Labour* has begun.

Gradually during labour the baby is pushed through the cervix, down the vagina and into the outside world.

After a few seconds the doctors and nurses clear the baby's nose and throat and the baby takes in his first breath — usually by crying! The umbilical cord — his lifeline up to now — can then be cut. It doesn't hurt him at all.

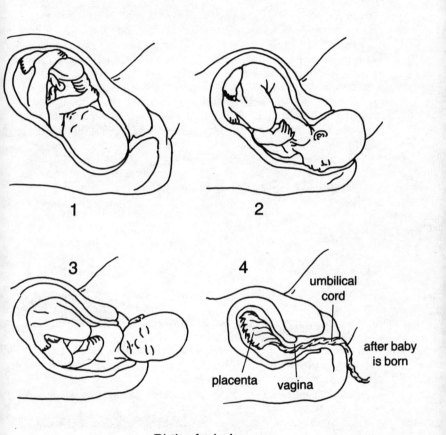

Birth of a baby

Birth is finished when the placenta with the cord attached separates from the wall of the uterus and is passed out through the vagina.

The whole birth process takes six to 12 hours on average. Ask your mum how long it took for you to be born.

Occasionally for one reason or another the mother has to have an operation to give birth to the baby. This is called a *Caesarean*. A cut is made in the mother's tummy and through the wall of the uterus. The baby is then lifted out, usually happy and ready to breathe! The mother, of course, is stitched up and a few days later is back on her feet.

Sometimes, because of slight problems, the baby needs extra care for a few days after birth. He will then be put immediately into a special care unit of the hospital. Because of this possibility, many doctors recommend women to have their babies in hospital rather than at home.

Birth can be quite a painful experience for the mother. (Look up Genesis 3 verse 16 and see how sin helped to cause this.) Modern drugs and learning to control breathing help to make the process a bit less painful. But every mother quickly forgets the pain when she holds her lovely baby for the first time.

Breast Milk

At about the time of birth, the mother's breasts start to produce a highly nutritious yellow liquid called *colostrum*. This feeds the baby for a couple of days as he sucks at his mother's breasts. It also helps to protect the newborn baby from infections.

Gradually the colostrum is replaced by milk, which is the baby's only source of food until he is *weaned* (starts to eat solid foods). The more he sucks, the more milk is produced.

A mother's milk looks more watery than cow's milk and has a slight bluish tinge.

If for some reason the mother is unable to breastfeed her baby — or chooses not to do so — the colostrum in her breasts disappears within a few days. Because the baby doesn't suck at her breasts, no milk is formed there.

God's Miracle

Every time a baby is born, a miracle takes place. A new little life, created by God to serve Jesus Christ, comes into the world.

Isn't it wonderful that God so carefully made each of us — with a bit of help from our mums and dads, of course!

Something to talk about

How would you tell someone who believes in abortion God's attitude towards the unborn baby? Spend some time right now thanking God for the way *you* were made in your mother's uterus.

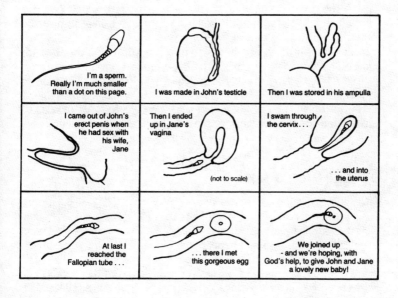

6

Your body grows up

When you were small you might have enjoyed reading about Peter Pan — the boy who never grew up — but the fact is that one day *you* will start getting an adult body if you haven't done so already. That's the growing stage called *puberty*.

It all starts in the head. (Seriously!) When you reach the time for puberty, part of the brain called the *hypothalmus* sends a message to the *pituitary,* a gland about the size of a pea located at the base of your brain.

The pituitary then sends a chemical message to your ovaries or testicles and your body begins the most dramatic change it will probably ever experience.

Changes for a Girl

Once puberty begins, the girl's ovaries produce an egg every month or so until she reaches the age of about 40 to 50.

At the same time, the uterus wall begins to prepare to receive a fertilised egg. If this doesn't happen, the blood-rich lining of the uterus breaks away and the girl's period begins.

For a few days, this blood passes very slowly out of the vagina. The girl wears a pad (*sanitary towel,* known as 'ST') or *tampon* to absorb the blood. A period doesn't usually hurt but occasionally the girl may have a tummy-ache. She also may not be able to go swimming or do certain other things.

There are other changes for the girl at puberty. Her hips become more rounded and her legs shapely.

Her breasts begin to enlarge (which sometimes causes a bit of pain) and quite quickly she will need to wear a bra.

Hair (called *pubic hair*) begins to grow around the vulva area between the legs and (later) under the arms.

Within just a few months, the girl has developed a young woman's body.

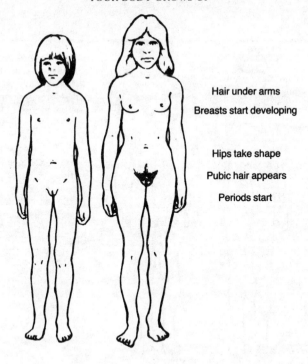

Hair under arms

Breasts start developing

Hips take shape

Pubic hair appears

Periods start

Before and after puberty

Changes for a Boy

Once the testicles of a boy have been stirred into action by the chemical messengers, they produce millions of sperm cells every day until he's an old man.

These sperm cells move through tubes (the vas deferens) and are stored in the ampulla (storage chamber) ready for use. When the chamber is full, the sperm cells must be removed for the new ones being produced to take their place.

Some are absorbed into the body but most are passed out through the end of the penis. For an unmarried young man, these sperm are removed naturally by nocturnal emissions or artificially by masturbating (the boy playing with himself sexually). We'll talk about masturbation in a later chapter.

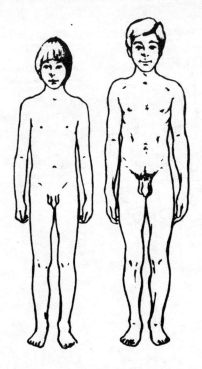

Whiskers develop
Voice deepens
Shoulders broaden
Hair under arms
Stronger muscles

Pubic hair appears
Penis and testicles
enlargen
Sperm cells form
Nocturnal emissions begin

Before and after puberty

When a boy reaches puberty, he will notice a number of other changes. The first sign is usually pubic hair starting to grow just above his penis. Later he will have hair in other places as well, including under the arms, on his face (whiskers) and — possibly — on his chest as well.

His penis and testicles will become much, much larger, his shoulders broader and his muscles more like those of a man.

His voice will break and be much deeper than before. As this begins to happen, he may find his voice changing from a high-pitched squeak to a deep growl — all in the same sentence!

Occasionally he might also have what are called 'growing pains' in his chest and joints. These go away after a time.

Hurry Up, Puberty!

Most young people are desperate to be more grown up. Girls look forward to wearing their first bra and becoming more shapely. Boys want to bc tougher and more manly looking. These are perfectly natural desires.

Most girls reach puberty a bit before boys. For many it happens between the ages of 11 and 13, although girls may enter puberty as young as 9 or 10 or as old as 16 or 17.

The average age for boys reaching puberty is 12 to 14. But it is not unusual for puberty to happen anywhere from the ages of 10 to 18!

There is nothing you can do to change the age of puberty. Located in your brain and pituitary gland is a kind of calendar that is set to begin the changes at a certain time. That's the way God made you.

Write down in your own words what Ecclesiastes 3 verse 1 says

about times of life. _____

_____

_____

Reaching puberty before all your friends can be a bit embarrassing. But if you develop much later than them, it can seem like the end of the world.

The fact is, though, that it *will* happen to you one day. How many adults do you know who still have the body of a child?! But if you're really worried, have a chat with your doctor. That's what he's there for.

Fit and Healthy

If you're a Christian, what has your body become (1 Corinthians 6

verse 19)? _____

_____

_____

Because that is true, you need to take care of your body, especially around puberty.

At this time you need to eat the right kinds of food. Avoid always having junk food and try to concentrate more on foods containing lots of protein, fibre and vitamins.

Make sure you don't eat too much greasy, sweet or salty food. This makes sense right through life.

Almost everyone at this time gets *spots* (or *pimples)* on their face and, less often, on the upper part of the body. This is because the skin starts producing an oily substance that can become infected and sometimes blocks the skin pores. This can cause young people a lot of embarrassment, although it's perfectly normal to have spots.

If you suffer badly from this problem, your doctor or chemist will probably be able to give you some sort of medicine to help. But you can help yourself by keeping your skin clean.

At puberty your sweat glands will come fully into use. That means making sure you wash regularly, especially under your arms and in the area of your sex organs. If you don't bother, you'll start smelling. Then all your friends might decide to stay away from you!

This isn't the time to go on silly diets like some of your friends. If you think you're a little on the plump side, try to eat more vegetables and fresh fruit, cut down on cakes and sweets and get more exercise. Diets for young people — especially girls — can be very dangerous unless they're advised by a doctor for medical reasons.

The Bible says that exercise has some profit (1 Timothy 4 verse 8). You don't have to be a champion athlete to be fit. Try a bit more walking, cycling, swimming or running. Take up tennis, cricket, badminton, football or hockey. Anything will do as long as you keep at it.

Smoking, drugs, glue sniffing and too much alcohol all harm your body so avoid them like the plague.

It might surprise you but at puberty you need more sleep than you did before! Instead of being grumpy all the time, try to get to bed a bit earlier and sleep in for a couple of hours on Saturdays and during school holidays.

You'll need that extra sleep. But don't use it as an excuse for being a layabout. The book of Proverbs has a lot to say about such people. Look up Proverbs 6 verses 6 to 11; 10 verse 26; 13 verse 4; 20 verse 4; and 26 verses 13 to 15. Now write down the one word that could sum up the people mentioned in all these verses. _____

We hope you'll manage to come through puberty without too many problems and become a young man or woman eager and ready to take your place in society.

Something to talk about

Without reading this chapter again, see if you can say what changes will happen to you when you reach puberty. Which ones are you most worried about — if any? If you've already started to mature sexually, explain instead what has been the most difficult thing to cope with.

7

Coping with change

In the last chapter we talked about the changes you can expect in your body as you reach puberty. But puberty is also a very *emotional* time.

New Feelings

Take Wendy, for instance. Wendy burst into tears for the tenth time that day. 'What's wrong with me, Mum?' she sobbed. 'I think I'm going mad!'

It wasn't long before Wendy's mum realised what was happening and was able to help her daughter. Crying for no apparent reason and being unusually emotional are often normal, healthy signs that a girl is about to enter puberty — and she will probably soon have her first period.

Girls — and boys, too — go through a lot of other feelings and emotions as they leave their childhood and start to develop adult bodies.

The few years after puberty are usually called *adolescence*. Being an adolescent is sometimes difficult. It will probably be the most emotional time you'll ever experience.

Every feeling you have — fears, pleasures, frustrations and annoyances — will seem so much bigger. And coping with them can be a problem.

You will find yourself falling madly in love. Just as easily, you'll probably fall out of love again.

During this time emotions often come in cycles, such as deep despair followed by extreme happiness. This can result in young people deciding things too quickly, without thinking them through first. We've even heard of a few who have suddenly and very foolishly turned to murder or suicide simply because they've had a miserable day!

Many of these emotions are the result of the extra large amounts of *hormones* (chemical messengers) that are produced at puberty (though that's no excuse for doing wrong). But some are simply part of putting childish things behind us as we grow up (see 1 Corinthians 13 verse 11).

New Freedom

Every adolescent goes through a time of no longer wanting to be tied
to his (or her) mother's apron strings or be 'mummy's baby'. He wants
to let go and begin to be independent.

The desire to become independent in this sense is part of God's plan
for every adolescent. But parents sometimes find it difficult to let go
a bit and young people foolishly want to be totally free to make all
their own decisions straightaway.

Jesus set the best example in this area. When he was 12, he was
taken by Mary and Joseph to Jerusalem for a special celebration of
thanks that he would soon leave the world of childhood and become
a young man. Modern Jews call this celebration the boy's *Bar Mitzvah*.

Read about it in Luke 2 verse 41 to 52. After Jesus went back to
Nazareth with Mary and Joseph, what was his attitude to them (verse

51)? _____

_____

Is that going to be your attitude to *your* parents? _____

New Faith

In verse 52 it says that during his teen years Jesus _____

_____ .

Adolescence is a time when young people often discover their *own*
relationship with God. Many give their lives to Jesus Christ for the
first time.

Others, who have been brought up in Christian families, come into
a new understanding of spiritual commitments they made in childhood.
Many are baptised in the Holy Spirit — and in water — and enter
whole new areas of gifts of the Spirit and learning to pray for the
healing, deliverance and salvation of others.

It's an exciting time!

New Pressures

But, as we've said before, being an adolescent is not all joy and
happiness. Most adolescents are tempted to do almost anything to be
like their friends. This is called *conformity*.

Conformity is another word for 'following the crowd'. You've
probably been tempted to copy what your friends do since you were

very young. Now, though, the pressure to conform will be even stronger.

It's difficult to be different. But that's so often what God wants. Read Matthew 7 verses 13 to 14 about the two roads of life. If you're

a Christian, which one are you on? _____

_____ Which one are most of your friends on?

_____

How about you showing how mature you are by refusing to conform with the crowd? Dare to be different! Show your friends that you're growing into a mature young man or young woman by not copying everything they do. Set a lead yourself — a new and better one — by living God's way.

New Body

When a young person reaches puberty, he becomes much more aware of his body. Boys often get stronger and better at sport. Girls become shapely and may be surprised at how attractive they are to boys!

But that new body can cause some real problems, especially in the school changing-room. You are very conscious of your body and yet you have to reveal yourself to all your friends.

It's doubly difficult for the one whose body hasn't matured yet — while most of his classmates' bodies have!

The truth is that anyone else in the same situation has the same embarrassment. If you don't believe us, ask a friend who you know will give an honest answer. If you feel inferior anyway, the problem becomes even worse.

Knowing that everyone else has the same embarrassment doesn't solve the problem — but it certainly helps!

New Attitudes

Once a young person reaches puberty, he is thrust out of childhood into a whole new world. Suddenly, he is tempted to feel very inferior, unimportant and insecure.

He looks around him and thinks: 'I just don't seem to have any real friends.' Or: 'I'm so ugly with all these spots.' Or: 'I'm really stupid compared with the others.' Or: 'I wish my parents had a bit more money — it's so embarrassing not to be able to afford things.'

James Dobson, in his superb book, *Preparing for Adolescence*

(Kingsway), calls this a lack of self-esteem. We strongly recommend that you get a copy of this book for yourself.

In it he says that the first step in dealing with low self-esteem is to realise that you're not alone. For instance, he found that eight out of ten teenagers dislike their appearance. Whatever problem you have in this area, face up to it fairly and squarely.

Then he suggests making up for your weak areas by concentrating on your strengths, finding true friends who will be honest with you and sharing your worries and fears with an adult (such as a parent or church leader — or a leader's wife) who understands the problems of young people.

Many of the great men in the Bible had this problem of inferiority and tried to use it as an excuse.

Among the reasons Moses gave for not obeying God was that he

was no good at _____
(Exodus 4 verse 10). What did God say about this (verse 12)?

_____

_____

After successfully challenging the prophets of the idol, Baal (1 Kings 18 verses 20 to 40), Elijah went and hid in a cave. He felt so lonely (19 verse 14), but God told him that there were still

_____ people in the land who had remained faithful to God and had not bowed to Baal (verse 18).

Jeremiah said that he couldn't be a prophet because he was too

_____ (Jeremiah 1 verses 4 to 6).
Write down what God said in reply (verses 7 to 8). _____

_____

_____

Right through adolescence we're confident that God will be with *you*, too.

Something to talk about

How would you help a young person who suddenly decides one day that life isn't worth living anymore? If you've reached puberty, explain how you deal with your emotions. Which of them do you find the most difficult?

8

Specially for girls

written by Christine Day

This chapter is just for the girls about a few things that really won't interest the boys. The boys can read it if they like, but they may find all this 'woman talk' a bit boring.

Bible Plan

Before we get down to some practical details, let's have a look at a few things that God wants you to be as a girl and young woman.

One of the best-known parts of the Bible about women is Proverbs 31 verses 10 to 31. Although it is about a married woman, most of it can apply to all young women — and older ones, too!

After you've read it, look at verses 17 and 25 again and write the one word used in both these verses to describe the godly woman:

_____

You can be strong in God, too (Ephesians 6 verse 10). This means that Jesus is able to give you peace when you're tempted to worry about the future or get upset about the smallest thing.

Ask him for the strength you need.

In Proverbs 31 verses 30 and 31 it says that beauty will disappear but the woman who 'honours the Lord' (puts God first in her life) should be praised. What does she deserve? _____

_____

Looking beautiful is very important to all of us women. But in 1 Timothy 2 verses 9 to 10 and 1 Peter 3 verses 3 to 4 it says that some things are much more important. What are they? _____

_____

_____

_____

As you grow in these areas, that inner beauty will show on your face.

God has promised it!

Finally, we women are often more easily deceived than men (see, for instance, 1 Timothy 2 verse 14). But God can help us to be wise instead of foolish. How do we get God's wisdom (James 1 verse 5)?

_____

_____

Pressure

Having said all that, I hope you don't think I'm trying to encourage you to be suddenly grown up in every way. One of the big problems for most girls is to be happy with how old they are and whether their bodies are developed or not.

There is pressure from TV, radio, magazines, comics and advertisements for girls to act and dress in a grown-up way before they're ready.

Adult fashion clothes and make-up are being produced for younger and younger girls. There is even make-up now that has been designed for girls aged six and seven!

God wants you to accept your age right now and not try to act grown-up (except in games) before you're there.

Taking Shape

Almost all girls look forward to having a figure and wearing a bra with pride. I hope you do!

It's a temptation to wear a bra before you're ready simply to be the same as your friends. I expect some of them will twist their mums' arms into buying one and then pad it out with tissues or cotton-wool. Imagine if, when they bent over, the padding fell out and the truth was known! How embarrassing.

I hope you'll never do that. Talk to your mum about buying a bra by all means, but don't try to force her when you're clearly not ready.

When the great day comes, don't go for the nicest bras in the shop. They can be very expensive and, because you'll develop quickly, they'll be too small in a few short months. Try to be sensible; I'm sure your parents aren't made of money.

You might be a bit shy about being measured for a bra by a shop assistant. Instead, why not get your mum to help you measure up at home? Then write the measurements on a piece of paper and hand it to the person in the shop.

You'll need to measure your chest under your bust next to your skin. This will give your *bra size*. Then measure round the fullest part of the bust and shoulder blades. The difference between the two will give you the *cup size* (usually labelled in the shop as AA, BB, etc).

Most shops sell an adjustable first-size bra, smaller than AA, which might be even better for you to start off with.

Curse or Blessing?

The other main sign of growing up, periods, can cause girls a lot of unnecessary worries. Some really dread having their first period for various reasons. They talk of periods as 'the curse', even though periods are a part of God's plan for every woman.

You might be a bit squeamish about the sight of blood. Well, I'm sorry, but you'll just have to get used to it. Millions and millions of other young women have.

A common worry is to imagine that you'll be walking down the road and suddenly you'll start bleeding all over the place. Don't worry, this just *isn't* the way periods start.

Probably the first sign you'll notice is a spot of blood in your underpants (knickers) when you go to the toilet. Then you'll know that it's time to start using an absorbent pad to catch the blood flow over the next few days. (Make sure you have some in the house well before your first period.)

Later on, when you've had a few periods, you may get to know when yours is due. Some girls get slight tummy pains or feel a bit sick. Others feel hungrier than usual or want to go to the toilet more often. Everyone is different so you'll have to find out for yourself.

While on the subject of periods, if yours are very painful, your doctor or chemist will probably be able to give you something to relieve the symptoms.

What Pad?

Another worry is about what kind of absorbent pads to use. As I expect you already know, there are two kinds: *sanitary towels* (usually called 'STs') and *tampons*.

An ST is rectangular in shape, usually with a sticky patch on one side covered by a peel-off strip. You simply pull off the strip, hold the other side in position against your skin and pull up your underpants. The patch sticks to your underpants, holding the ST in place. (It's even simpler to do than describe!)

Getting rid of a used ST is just as simple. Tear the back off (or pull off a tab on the back) and flush both parts down the toilet. Some school and public toilets have special bins to put the used STs in. Those are then burnt rather than flushed away.

The main disadvantages of STs are that you can't go swimming while you're wearing them and that they might show if you wear tight-fitting trousers or a leotard.

A tampon is about the size and shape of a small cigar. A packet comes with a small cardboard applicator to push the tampons up into your vagina. All that shows is a thin piece of cotton or thin string so that you can pull the used tampon out and flush it down the toilet.

Tampons are designed to help a woman lead as normal a life as possible during her period. She can do almost anything, including swim, with a tampon in place.

They are, however, a bit more difficult to use than STs. Some girls find them uncomfortable and they can lead to certain serious infections if they are left in for too long.

My advice is to start off with STs at least until you get used to having periods. Then see how you get on with tampons. Keep some STs handy as well in case it doesn't work out.

While I'm on the subject of absorbent pads, it's important to think ahead. Whatever pad you use, make sure you always have a supply. Carry one or two with you if you can. Some companies make a special plastic case that would fit any handbag or schoolbag.

If your period starts at school and you are caught out, tell the school nurse or secretary. She'll probably be able to help. But if the worst comes to the worst, you could use a few tissues or pieces of toilet paper temporarily.

Some girls get very worried that their periods are a bit irregular. Others wonder why their periods last longer or shorter than a week. Still others are concerned because their periods don't happen exactly every 28 days, which is the average.

At first, your periods are bound to be a bit irregular until your body gets used to them. Also, everyone has their own unique 'body clock', so there is no point in worrying if you're not average.

Should you ever have any worries about your periods, talk to your doctor who, occasionally, might recommend medicine to get your body clock regular.

Future Worries

Girls sometimes have serious worries about what sex will be like when they get married. They may have heard stories about husbands being brutal during sex on the wedding night and of wives bleeding because of it.

Many of these misleading stories come because some girls don't understand about the hymen. As we've discovered already, the hymen partly covers the opening of the vagina in an unmarried girl or woman. Occasionally, it stretches or tears during sport or horseriding or through the use of tampons, but generally it is the God-given sign of a virgin.

Usually, the first time a wife has sex, the hymen stretches fully open. This can cause a small amount of bleeding and, possibly, some pain. But this is quickly forgotten in the joy of discovering each other's body in a permanent marriage relationship.

Many women, just before getting married, go to see their doctor for a check-up. Occasionally, if the hymen is particularly tough, the doctor may stretch it open fully during this check-up to make sex easier and more enjoyable for the woman on her wedding night.

It's as simple as that! If you've heard untrue rumours, don't believe them anymore.

Body Beautiful

Finally, remember as you grow up that the sight of your body will become more and more attractive to boys and men. There's nothing wrong with that. Just be careful not to wear things that deliberately cause them sexual temptations. You may be asking for problems!

Think before you buy very tight-fitting or low-cut fashionable clothes. Give away or throw out shorts and swimming costumes that are now too small for you. And, above all, remember to sit properly!

Something to talk about

What worries do you have about periods? In what ways can a period be a blessing instead of 'the curse'?

Christine Day

Specially for boys

written by Roger Day

It's about time that we had a chat together, man to man, about a few things that have nothing to do with the women. Of course, the girls may want to have a sneaky read of this chapter, but it won't mean much to them.

Bible Plan

Before we talk about some of the practical things that worry many young men, let's have a look at what the Bible teaches about growing into manhood.

By far the best example of manliness in the Bible is Jesus himself. When he was still a young boy, it says in Luke 2 verse 40 that he

grew and became _____ .

He was also full of _____

_____ .

After he reached the age of 12, he continued to grow in three areas.

What were they (verse 52)? _____

_____

_____

It wasn't just that his body was getting stronger, but he was learning to be stronger in his attitudes. He was a young man who promised to do something — and did it. He learned to have courage, determination and boldness. He was a boy who could be *trusted*.

Having God's wisdom doesn't necessarily mean being the cleverest person in your class at school (see 1 Corinthians 3 verses 18 to 20). Instead it means knowing what God wants in every area of your life. How do you get that kind of wisdom (James 1 verse 5)?

_____

_____

Jesus set us the example of a real man when he showed how determined he was to put God first in everything he did. He was brave enough to chase the moneylenders from the temple (John 2 verses 13 to 17). He had courage to tell the religious leaders what God really thought of them (Matthew 23 verses 27 to 28). And he showed boldness to stand against Satan when he was tempted to sin (Matthew 4 verse 1 to 11).

But Jesus wasn't a hard man without feelings. He had love for the sinful people of Jerusalem (Matthew 23 verse 37). He showed care and concern for his mother when he was about to die (John 19 verses 26 to 27). And he cried after his friend, Lazarus, died (John 11 verses 32 to 36).

If you look at some pop stars and others on TV you can see examples of men who have chosen to act and dress in a very unmanly way. I challenge you to follow Jesus' manly example instead.

Being Different

God has very carefully made each one of us. Yet a lot of boys and young men have all kinds of worries and fears about their sex organs.

Some boys have only one testicle. If you're one of them and haven't talked to your doctor about it yet, it's time you did. Sometimes one testicle stays stuck inside the boy's body above his penis and doesn't descend into the scrotum. A small operation can often pull it down into its proper place with the other.

But even if your doctor can't help you, there's no need to worry. I have a friend with one testicle who is married with a number of children. He is a real man's man — and he certainly doesn't have any sexual difficulties!

Some boys have a penis that is different from those of their friends. They might be very embarrassed about this, especially if their friends keep laughing at them. In fact, they might be so embarrassed about it that they haven't asked their parents why they're different.

The usual difference is that some boys have been circumcised while most others haven't. If you're not sure, look at the two drawings below and decide which drawing your penis is most like. (There are always minor differences so don't worry if the drawing you choose isn't exactly the same!)

Circumcision is usually done on a boy when he is very young. The small flap of skin (the prepuce, or foreskin) that covers the end of the penis is cut away leaving the end exposed.

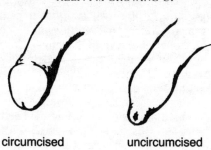

circumcised   uncircumcised

There are three reasons why this is done. The most common is that the flap of skin is too tight to pull back completely so that the glans can be cleaned. This can lead to pain and discomfort.

The second reason is that some parents think a circumcised penis is more hygienic than one that hasn't been circumcised. This is one of those views that changes every few years.

It's true that, if you're not circumcised, it's important especially after puberty to pull the skin back every week or so to wash away the dead skin and white soapy substance, called *smegma,* that collects there (making sure, of course, that you move the skin back afterwards). This can be done each time you have a bath or shower, using water but no soap. But being circumcised or not really doesn't make much difference.

The third reason for being circumcised is religious. All Jewish and Muslim boys have the operation as babies. And, because Jesus was born a Jew, he was circumcised. How old was he when this was done

(Luke 2 verse 21)? _____

You don't need to be circumcised to be a Christian, though! See Galatians 5 verse 6.

If you *are* circumcised, don't worry. It doesn't make any difference to having children, enjoying sex — or going to the toilet!

Another common worry among boys is that, when their penis is erect, it is a bit crooked or bends in one direction or the other. Don't worry; it will make little or no difference to sexual enjoyment.

'I Can't Help It!'

Quite a few boys, after they reach puberty, find that they occasionally have an erection and then pass sperm out of their penis during the daytime without touching themselves, almost like a nocturnal emission.

It can happen at the most unusual of times — in class or church meetings or even watching a football match.

This is called a *spontaneous ejaculation.* If you have them from time to time, don't worry — you're perfectly normal. If you *don't* ever have them, there's nothing wrong with you, either!

Another thing that happens to a lot of boys is that, after their penis has been erect for some time, a couple of drops of clear sticky fluid comes out of the end. This happens to all boys and men, though many might not even notice it. The fluid neutralises the acid in the urine so that when the sperm cells pass through the penis they aren't harmed. Again, don't worry!

Embarrassing Miracle

One of God's miracles is the way a penis can become erect almost at a moment's notice. An erection is essential for sex, as we've already learnt. But it can sometimes be embarrassing when it happens at other times, especially in changing-rooms and at swimming pools!

Even a very young boy can have an erect penis. It usually means that he needs to go to the toilet and if his mother doesn't do something quickly, she could get a warm shower!

As he gets older, the boy finds that he has erections for other reasons — touching his penis, wearing tight clothes, when he wakes up in the morning, after a swim or shower or allowing himself to think sexual thoughts. Quite often he'll have an erection for no apparent reason when he least expects it.

Some boys get very worried about this. But there is absolutely nothing to be ashamed of. It's completely natural and normal.

You might worry that you'll have an erection when you're in the school changing-room or when you're being looked at by a doctor. First, remember that everyone else has the same worry, as we've already mentioned.

Second, the more you worry and concentrate on *not* having an erection, the more likely it is to happen. (If you don't believe me, close your eyes and try not to think of elephants. I'm sure that, because you're trying not to, you'll think of them all the time!)

Even if the worst happened and you had an erection, it wouldn't really matter. It's so common that I expect even a woman doctor wouldn't take much notice.

If it happened in the changing-room and someone laughed, you could make a joking remark like: 'It happens to *real* men, you know.' But don't be unkind to other boys about their sex organs — even in fun.

Sometimes you might have an erection when you're sitting in class or watching TV. It might be tempting to start touching or playing with yourself when this happens. My advice is: 'Don't.'

If you do, you might start drawing attention to yourself. Anyway, learning to control yourself now is good preparation for facing the bigger battles with masturbation later.

When you have an erection, wherever you are, quickly move your penis into a comfortable position if you have to and then leave it alone. It'll soon be back to its normal size again. That way, it's likely that no one else will notice, even if you're only wearing swimming trunks.

Self-Control

Finally, remember that many sexual temptations for young men begin with the eyes. Learn to control what you look at: TV, videos, books, pictures and magazines. Jesus said that a man who looks with lust

at a girl or woman has already _____

_____

_____ (Matthew 5 verses 27 to 28).

Someone has said about sexual temptation: 'You can't help the first look, but the second look is sin.' Remember that — always.

Something to talk about

How would you help someone who was worried about having erections at embarrassing times? According to the Bible, what should a real man be like?

Roger Day

10

Small is beautiful!

Have you ever said: 'I hate my body'? Many people have. They think that, because they don't like parts of their body, they must have been made wrongly.

But God wants you to accept yourself just the way you are. Read Psalm 139 verses 1 to 18 and see some of the things that God says there about his love for you.

How much of you did God make (verse 13)? _____

When did he first know you (verses 15 to 16)? _____

Not only that, God says that you are chosen, carefully made and precious. (See Ephesians 2 verses 4 to 10; 1 John 3 verses 1 to 2; and 1 Peter 2 verses 9 to 10.) He knew what he was doing when he made you and he wants you to accept that fact and love yourself, even through the difficult years of adolescence.

Sex Organs

Of course, it's easy to talk about accepting things like your height, looks, shape of teeth and colour of hair. But what about your sex organs?

You'd be surprised how many young people go through years of secret agony because they think that they haven't got the right sexual equipment.

Boys and young men often think their penis must be too small to have sex. A few might even feel that it may be too big, though they probably wouldn't admit to thinking that way!

Girls usually have the most worries about the size of their breasts. Those with large breasts tend to think these should be smaller, especially if they get teased a lot by the boys at school. Those with very small breasts worry themselves silly because theirs are smaller than those of their friends.

Some older girls start to wonder if their vagina is too short or narrow or if their clitoris is too small to enjoy sex properly.

Let's make it quite clear. God knew what he was doing when he made you. And by the time you leave your teen years, your body will almost certainly be ready sexually.

Confusing Ideal

One of the problems is that TV, newspapers, magazines and even books have decided what the 'ideal' man and woman should look like. If a man's swimming trunks aren't bulging in the right place or a woman isn't 'busting out all over', they make you think you're odd or inferior.

One example of this happened not very long ago. A survey showed that the average bust size of British women had increased. The popular newspapers used headlines like: 'Britain's beauties are busting out' and: 'Breasts are getting BIGGER.' They gave the impression that, if you were less than average, you were missing out. How wrong they were!

Another common pressure area for younger girls is the image given by 'grown-up' dolls such as Sindy and Barbie. They give the totally wrong impression that every girl after puberty becomes absolutely glamorous, with long sexy legs, 'perfect' figure and clear unblemished skin.

When girls find that they aren't very attractive or are shorter than average or have spots, all their hopes and dreams can easily be shattered.

Positive Thinking

The truth is that God made every part of your body   _____

_____

(1 Corinthians 12 verse 18). How dare you question God's design and plan for you!

If you have real worries about your sexual equipment that go on for year after year, the best thing to do is to talk to your parents about it or — with their help if necessary — have a chat with your doctor.

Whatever you do, learn to think positively about this and every other area of life. Don't let society influence you by its impossible standards.

What, according to Romans 12 verse 2, should you do instead?

_____

_____

Now read Philippians 4 verses 8 and write down from there eight positive things to fill your mind with.

1 _____   2 _____

3 _____   4 _____

5 _____   6 _____

7 _____   8 _____

Begin to practise thinking positively about your body. God made you the way you are and he accepts you. No doubt, one day when you're grown up you'll find someone of the opposite sex who is deeply attracted to you and with whom you can share your life. But even if you don't and God calls you to a single life, you'll still be acceptable to your Maker.

Something to talk about

What parts of your body, if any, do you dislike? How can you learn to have a right attitude to them?

11

Masturbation: the lonely battle

If most young people were honest enough to admit their biggest problem with sex, they would probably say that it was *masturbation* — playing with their penis or vulva area to produce a pleasant feeling when no one else is about.

Masturbation is one of those subjects which people have different views about. In this chapter we'll be sharing with you *our* beliefs about it, though your parents may want to have their say on the subject, too.

Some young people take the view that masturbation is a fun part of life and not at all wrong. Some Christian young people, on the other hand, get so worried and upset about their problem with it that they even think of giving up living for Jesus. We believe that both attitudes are wrong.

First of all, masturbation — when it involves just you — is *not* one of those sexual sins that the Bible says are so very wrong and which lead to serious problems. Those sexual sins *always* involve more than one person.

Masturbation can, however, become a big nuisance. The Bible doesn't say anything about it, but it *does* say that everything that doesn't come from faith is sin (Romans 14 verse 23). In other words, if you masturbate without knowing that God approves of it, then to you it is wrong.

A lot of Christian young people — especially boys — who are winning victories for Jesus in many other ways, seem to keep losing the battle in this area.

Boys, in fact, have a much bigger problem with masturbation than girls. Someone once said that 99 out of every 100 adolescent boys say they have battles with masturbation — and the other one's a liar!

There are a number of reasons for this. Boys are more quickly stirred sexually; masturbation for them is easier than for girls; and — probably the main reason — once the boy reaches puberty his testicles start producing large amounts of sperm, which must be got rid of in one way or another.

Something like 500 million tiny sperm cells are made every day and these are stored ready for use. Of course, it's going to be a few years before the boy gets married. So each time the storage chamber (ampulla) is full, the body has to remove them to make room for more. It does this usually at night with a nocturnal emission, as we've already learnt.

But for the few days before that happens, the boy may be more easily excited sexually. He soon learns that, by masturbating, the sperm is passed out of his penis in quite an enjoyable way — and the cycle begins again.

Of course, boys might also be tempted to masturbate to a climax at other times. Each time they do masturbate in this way, semen is spurted out, though the more this happens the less the amount of semen that comes out.

In the case of boys who haven't yet reached puberty, masturbation eventually results in the same kind of 'tickly' or 'stinging' feeling but of course no semen is involved. At the beginning of puberty, a small amount of clear, sticky liquid is spurted out each time. This gradually changes to the white cloudy semen of the adolescent and adult.

With girls, masturbation can start accidentally, by rubbing themselves, or, more often, by being told the lie: 'Everyone else does it, so why not try?'

For both boys and girls, masturbation when it is continued to a climax can result in a very pleasant feeling. That's the side everyone who has done it would admit to. What people tend to forget is that it also often leads to frustration and disappointment.

You see, it's not God's plan for you so it's bound to be a bit like that. Fulfilling your sexual desires should be saved for when you get married and then be directed to your marriage partner (1 Corinthians 7 verses 1 to 4).

When you get married, your duty (and privilege) is to bring sexual pleasure to your husband or wife. Of course, it will also be very enjoyable for *you,* but this is God's bonus, not a right.

Sexual pleasure through masturbation on your own is selfish, self-centred and self-directed. It cuts across God's plan for you and is therefore not right.

Now let's imagine that in a couple of years' time you're having battles with masturbation. You've tried it a few times (most people do) and now, however hard you've tried to stop, it's become almost a habit. There are three possible ways of dealing with it:

1. Carry on Regardless

The first is to say: 'It's good fun. No one knows about it so I'll carry on. I won't even bother confessing it to God.'

Many non-Christian teachers and modern books on sex teach this. They say that masturbation can't harm you, which is true, although it can make your sexual organs a bit sore for a while if you do it a lot.

They also say that it is good practice for marriage — which is a total lie.

Someone who lets masturbation become a regular habit has only himself to think about. When he gets married, he needs to think about the needs of his partner. He might easily find this too much like hard work and carry on masturbating, which can lead to serious problems in the marriage.

Another thing is that, in marriage, there will be times when sex won't be possible for various reasons. If you let masturbation become a regular habit now, it will be much more difficult to control yourself during those times. So if you want to practise for marriage, practise *not* masturbating instead! You see, God wants us always to be in control of our actions. Look up Galatians 5 verses 22 to 23 and write

down the last part of the fruit of the Spirit. _____

Would uncontrolled masturbation help you to be that? _____

Although the Bible doesn't specifically say that masturbation is wrong, it does tell us: 'Be holy in all that you do, just as God who called you is holy' (1 Peter 1 verse 15). Can we imagine Jesus masturbating? No!

We are also told to offer our bodies to God as a _____

_____(Romans 12 verse 1). Now ask yourself

whether or not it's possible to do that and masturbate at the same time.

Another very important thing to remember is that masturbation is often linked with wrong, sinful thoughts, as we'll see in the next chapter.

On the other hand, uncontrolled masturbation can easily become *just a habit*. When that happens, if you don't have anything better to do, or can't sleep one night, you automatically start playing with yourself.

It can become a bit like biting your nails or thumb-sucking. If you knew someone your age who still sucked his thumb you'd probably tell him: 'It's about time you grew up.' Well, it's the same with this kind of masturbation.

2. Develop Guilt Feelings

The second way of dealing with masturbation is much more dangerous.

Imagine a young Christian person who is doing very well in this and other areas of his life. Suddenly, in a moment of weakness, he gets tempted and before he thinks twice he has masturbated.

Instead of confessing his sin to God and then forgetting about it, he starts feeling really guilty. He decides he's a no-good failure and gets extremely miserable.

He thinks: 'Because I've failed in this area, I can't be much use to God. I might as well give up living as a Christian altogether.'

Can you see what that person has done? He has let Satan fool him into thinking that God can't forgive him. What a lie! It's typical of

the devil, who is called the father of _____
(John 8 verse 44).

Don't ever let Satan fool *you* this way.

3. Confess and Forget

The third way of dealing with masturbation is God's way. It's the same as with other sins like lying, answering back to your teacher or getting impatient.

Look up 1 John 1 verses 8 to 10. If we *confess our sins* to God (in other words, tell God about them, be deeply sorry and turn from them),

what has he promised to do? _____

_____

God's way for you to deal with masturbation — and any other sin — is to confess it, tell God you're not going to do it again and then forget it. Don't keep count of how many times you've failed in the past — God certainly doesn't! He chooses to forget each time, sending our sins to the bottom of the sea, never to be seen again (Micah 7 verse 19).

Once you've confessed any sin, get on with living your Christian life. Live one day at a time instead of worrying about either yesterday or tomorrow. Satan's chief aim is to take away your peace. He'll no doubt try it in this area — but whatever you do, don't let him win.

Don't pretend you don't have a problem with masturbation if you do. Some people get into the habit of wriggling in bed to reach a climax. That's as much masturbation as using your hand. Admit it!

Finally, if masturbation isn't a big issue for you at the moment, or in the future, don't worry. There's nothing wrong with *not* having a problem!

Something to talk about

What advice would you give to someone who has a serious problem with masturbation? In what way is masturbation different from the sexual sin that the Bible talks about?

.

12

A fight for the mind

If you haven't reached puberty yet, you'll find it difficult to understand fully what a powerful thing sexual desire is. It's about the strongest attraction you'll ever experience. But, when it becomes very strong, always remember that God put that desire in you and he can help you to avoid the sin that comes from using it wrongly (see Jude verses 24 to 25).

Like other good gifts, Satan tries with everything he's got to turn sex into something harmful, bad and sinful. He constantly seems to put sexual temptations in the way of young (and older!) people.

'Come on,' he seems to whisper. 'Enjoy yourself just this once. None of your Christian friends is around. Only the two of you need ever know.'

Pure Thoughts

That might or might not be true. But God is always there and he knows every action. Not only that, but he is aware of every *thought* you think. And he wants your thought life to be pure, especially in the area of sex.

Jesus put it very strongly in Matthew 5 verse 28 when he said that any man who looks at a woman and in his mind wants her sexually has *already* committed sexual sin.

King David was a man after God's own heart (Acts 13 verse 22), yet he committed sexual sin with Bathsheba because he *looked* with his eyes and then allowed his *mind* to dwell on what he saw, helped by his *imagination*. This led eventually to *action* (2 Samuel 11 verses 1 to 27). What a tragedy for such a great man!

You, too, could easily go the same way if you were to allow your mind constantly to think the way it likes. Yet, if you know Jesus Christ as the Lord of your life and are being constantly filled with the Holy Spirit, you have what it takes to live in absolute victory and be an example to others of purity and right living. That's the way to have a happy marriage when the time comes.

You can make it and be a success!

Imagination needs to be controlled at its source — the eyes. A person sees someone of the opposite sex and his mind starts to desire that person sexually. Instead of quickly rejecting the thought in the name of Jesus, he allows his imagination to get up to all kinds of tricks.

That's when a simple wrong thought can so easily end up in action — and inevitable disaster.

Reject Rubbish

Even worse is reading rude books, looking at sexy pictures in newspapers and magazines or watching films, videos and TV programmes with a strong sexual content. The biggest trouble with this sort of thing (usually called *pornography)* is that it's very much like taking drugs — once you've started you're never satisfied and always keep coming back for more.

Some people, especially men, have fed themselves so much on this sort of rubbish that only the worst forms of pornography — sex involving violence *(sado-masochism),* animals *(bestiality),* several people *(group sex)* and young children *(paedophilia)* — can now satisfy them.

Surveys in the USA have proved how pornography can affect the way you think and act. Men in Alaska buy more sexy magazines than anywhere else in the USA, so it isn't surprising that Alaska also has the highest percentage of *rape* (forced sex) in the country.

Researchers have found that the more pornography a man looks at the more difficult he finds it is to control his thought life. Pornography wrecks marriages and convinces single people not to marry; it makes men want to try out the sinful things they look at; and it leads to a rise in rape, sex attacks on children, wife beatings and sex-related murders.

No wonder we urge you not to have anything to do with it. It is an evil disease that spreads like cancer in your mind.

In the same way, you need to be careful what books you borrow from the library. There are many, many books that show sex in a wrong kind of way and that are designed to stir the reader up sexually through what is written. Some are aimed specifically at young people. Don't get caught in the trap of reading this sort of thing.

Control Yourself

However strongly you are tempted to think rude and wrong thoughts,

you can have the power to say no. Look up 1 Corinthians 10 verse
13 and write it down here. _____

_____

_____

_____

_____

_____

_____

Now believe the truth of what you've written.

Sexual thoughts can, of course, easily lead to temptations to
masturbate. For many people, uncontrolled thoughts become a big
problem in bed as they let their minds go just before dropping off to
sleep.

Even here, you can be in control of your thoughts. Start thinking
good instead of evil, pray and praise God, speak in tongues or think
about some of the great things God has said in the Bible.

It takes practice to control your thinking but you *can* do it. Paul
says in 2 Corinthians 10 verse 5 that Christians can take captive every

thought and _____

_____

Accept the challenge!

Something to talk about

'In the area of sex, you can't help the way you think.' Talk about this
statement saying why you believe it to be wrong.

13

'I think I'm gay'

Homosexuality is a big problem today. One of the questions a growing number of young people are asking is: 'Am I gay?' One teenage boy wrote to a daily newspaper saying: 'I thought I was gay, but now I have very strong feelings for a girl.'

Older people, too, are asking similar questions. A woman wrote to a Christian magazine saying: 'I so much want to fall in love, get married and have a family — but I'm attracted to women, not men . . . . Is it truly wrong?'

Even if *you* don't have questions like that, it's important that you understand the correct attitude to these things. So please read on!

What It Means

The word 'gay' used to mean merry, bright, joyful, lively, carefree and cheerful. Now people use it mainly to describe a man who engages in sexual acts with other men, or a woman with other women (often called *lesbian* acts)

We prefer to use the proper word for this kind of sin, *homosexual* rather than 'gay'. We suggest you do as well.

Homosexuals are certainly nothing new. They have been around in every society since the beginning. It's just that, when a nation becomes increasingly evil, more of its people deliberately choose to turn to homosexuality. So it's not surprising that more and more young people today are wondering if they really belong to the homosexual community.

The Bible talks about this increase in homosexual activity happening in the city of Sodom. Read Genesis 19 verses 1 to 26 and see how strongly God felt about the homosexual sin, sexual *perversion* and other evil there.

God says in Leviticus 20 verse 13: 'If a man has sexual relations with another man, they have done a disgusting thing, and both shall be put to death.'

Thankfully, God doesn't demand the same punishment for a homosexual today! But that verse shows just how wrong homosexual sin is. (See also Leviticus 18 verse 22 and 1 Timothy 1 verses 9 to 11.)

The Result

Now read Romans 1 verses 18 to 27. What do people worship when they have given themselves over to evil (verse 25)? _____

_____

When people deliberately choose to commit homosexual sin, what sort of punishment do they receive (verse 27)? _____

_____

_____

What do you think this means?_____

_____

_____

Homosexual sin is wrong because God says it's wrong. He made each man for a woman and each woman for a man (Genesis 2 verses 22 to 24). Only in a marriage relationship with one person of the *opposite* sex can anyone find real, lasting and growing sexual satisfaction.

What It Causes

People who commit homosexual sin have always had a big battle against the various sexually transmitted diseases (STD) which, as you know, are spread by sexual contact. But in the last ten years a new disease has appeared — AIDS — which up to recently has been spread mainly by homosexuals and is closely linked to the practice of *sodomy* (using the anus — back passage — as a pretend vagina).

AIDS — acquired immune deficiency syndrome — destroys the body's ability to fight disease. Most of the people who catch it die a horrible death within a few short years.

AIDS has already resulted in thousands of deaths in the USA and hundreds more in Britain and other parts of Europe. Innocent people, including children, have suffered because of blood transfusions or possibly even organ transplants from people with AIDS.

Drug addicts can catch it by using dirty syringes to inject themselves with. Some people with haemophilia, who need a lot of blood products, have caught it from infected supplies.

Some women have caught the disease by having sex with men who are sexually attracted to both men and women *(bisexuals)* and who have sex with both. If they then have sex with other *heterosexuals* (people who are attracted to those of the opposite sex), AIDS can infect almost anyone who commits sexual sin.

As a result AIDS has spread much wider than the homosexual community, although the person who doesn't have sex outside of marriage is very unlikely to catch it.

Attempts have been made to stop the spread of AIDS. People are being told to have only one sexual partner. (The Bible tells us that, too!) Men are urged to use condoms if they have more than one partner of either sex. This might help in some cases, but, particularly with homosexual sin, AIDS can spread despite this precaution.

Quite often women with the disease, or who are carriers of it, have children who are born with AIDS. Then, as they grow up, people keep away from them because of fear of catching the disease. How sad!

Many people believe that God has allowed AIDS to appear to show his hatred of sexual sin, particularly homosexual acts. Whether you believe that or not, the fact is that at the moment scientists all over the world are desperately working on a cure for AIDS. But it will be years before victims of it can hope to receive effective treatment.

Meanwhile, many people, including large numbers of homosexuals, will die from it. The lives of many thousands more family and friends of victims will be devastated as a result. We can't break God's loving rules and get away with it.

Good News

The exciting news is that even the worst homosexual can become a Christian by repenting of (turning away from) his sin and receiving Jesus Christ into his life.

In 1 Corinthians 6 verses 9 to 11 Paul lists various types of sinners, including homosexuals, and says: 'Some of you were like that. But you have been purified from sin; you have been dedicated to God; you have been put right with God by the Lord Jesus Christ and by the Spirit of our God.' Isn't that great news?

A Real Problem

Real homosexuals are fairly rare. Although it is claimed (probably wrongly) that a quarter of the population of the USA have some form of 'homosexual orientation', only about four per cent are completely homosexual. Four per cent is probably about the proportion of homosexuals in Britain, too.

Homosexuals usually have one or more problems in their past that have resulted in their present desires. Many had a weak father and a mother who ruled the home. Others felt rejected as children because their parents wanted a child of the opposite sex — and may even have dressed them up as the boy or girl they really wanted.

A few others may be the way they are because of a frightening sexual experience in their early childhood.

Recent research has shown that a homosexual is still like a child, desperately searching for a relationship that was lost in his early years.

But whatever resulted in a person becoming a homosexual, he can be set free by the power of Jesus Christ. It will take prayer, time and discipline as well as help from Christian leaders — but many former homosexuals are now happily married with families of their own.

Going Astray

When any society begins to become corrupt, the people in it deliberately turn their backs on normal God-given sex and seek unnatural relations. The evil men of Gibeah wanted to commit homosexual sin with a man visiting the town. When they were denied that, they spent the night raping and abusing a young girl (Judges 19 verses 22 to 25).

The men of Sodom were a bit like that, too, as we've already seen. That's what corruption does. People *deviate* from their normal, healthy sexual desires to lust after those of their own sex — or even animals!

Sometimes people living in homosexual sin claim to be Christians. They might sing the same songs as those who know Jesus Christ as Lord, but they are living in sin as much as an unmarried man and woman having sex with each other. And they need to repent and stop their sinful acts.

These so-called homosexual 'Christians' often use Romans 1 verses 18 to 32 to say that it is only those who *choose* to deviate who are wrong. This of course isn't true. *All* homosexual sin is wrong. But Romans 1 is an important chapter and should be studied carefully.

Experimenting

Young people around the age of puberty — or a little before it — may go through a stage when they are more interested in those of their own sex. This is a normal, healthy part of growing up and usually passes very quickly.

Sometimes, during this stage, there may be a bit of experimenting — touching or masturbating with each other (*mutual masturbation*). This is of course very wrong and, if you've done it, you need to say sorry to God and stop doing it. It may also be helpful to talk to parents about it.

But such experimenting does *not* mean that a person is a homosexual. In fact, a survey conducted many years ago showed that 50 per cent of boys 'play around' before they reach puberty. Today that figure might be even higher.

Unfortunately, this phase was once unwisely labelled the 'homosexual phase'. In the last few years homosexual teachers (and well-meaning ones with normal ['heterosexual'] desires) have convinced young people going through it that they must be homosexual.

If *you've* been told that, you can either believe the lie of one or two people or you can accept the truth that God made you to look forward to normal, enjoyable sex with someone of the opposite sex in a happy, exciting marriage relationship.

Let's make it perfectly clear. You are *not* a homosexual simply because:

1. You once experimented

After all, you don't suddenly develop four wheels and an engine if you spend the night in a garage!

2. You don't go out with people of the opposite sex

Some people are far too busy studying or enjoying sport to spend their time going out with one person after another. Don't worry if you're not yet ready for having a boyfriend or girlfriend. Your time *will* come.

3. *You might not think you're very attractive/handsome*

God designed you just the way you are, including your looks. He also wants the best for you. Almost certainly, in due time, the right person will come along.

Desire and Action

It's very important to understand the difference between committing homosexual sin and the desire to do so. This desire is usually called *homosexual orientation* or *tendency*.

The sin is wrong, but the desire, while it isn't God's best for a person's life, comes into the area of temptation, and temptation isn't sin. All of us face temptations of one kind or another almost every day. It's only when we give in to the temptation, and so sin, that it becomes wrong.

So in God's eyes there isn't a lot of difference between the person who has homosexual temptations and the one who is tempted to commit sexual sin with the opposite sex. If you know someone who has homosexual temptations, don't condemn him (or her). But you could pray for him!

Between the homosexual sex act and the desire is a middle area of non-sexual activity. People with strong homosexual desires may be tempted to dress, speak and behave like those of the opposite sex. They may enjoy mixing with friends who have the the same desires. These things are never helpful and can easily lead into sin. Avoid them.

If you end up having homosexual desires, it's not the end of the world. God can work in your life as much as in anyone else's, providing you refuse to commit sexual sin. And hopefully one day, with your Maker's help, you will find that your thoughts and desires will switch gradually towards those of the opposite sex. Why not believe God that you will have a happy married life?

Meanwhile, keep yourself free from sin in this area and don't let anyone say that you are somehow second-class because of your desires.

Positive Steps

There is no doubt that homosexuals are attracting more public attention today. Young people, especially Christians, need to take their stand against homosexual sin in all its various forms.

At the same time, it's easy to condemn homosexuals instead of seeing them as people made by God who need to know his love and power in their lives. Christians can make a clear stand against their sinful acts — but we can be different from many people around us by showing loving concern for them.

It should really be a case of *hating the sin* but *loving the sinner*.

For yourself, actively seek to develop manly or womanly characters. Boys, be real young men. Girls, become lovely young ladies. Look at adults around you whom you really admire and seek to be like them in these areas.

Avoid homosexual or bisexual fashions and anything else (such as hairstyle) that makes it difficult for others to tell if you're a girl or a boy. (There's nothing wrong with trousers or a tracksuit for a girl — as long as she still looks like a girl.)

With God's help you can be an example to those around you of how a young man or woman ought to live.

Something to talk about

Pretend that a 13-year-old friend of yours tells you that he (or she) thinks he's a homosexual (or she's a lesbian). What sort of things would you say to help your friend?

14

Watch what you wear

One problem today is how far you can go in wearing the latest fashion. It's great to look good and to keep up with the latest trends (if your parents can afford it!), but there are a number of danger areas.

The fact is that many fashionable clothes are designed by evil men who go out of their way to make a girl highly sexually attractive to men and boys. In addition, some boys' fashions are designed by homosexuals to attract attention to the body. You're asking for trouble if you wear any of these.

Right or Wrong?

So how do you decide what's right and what's not in the area of fashion? In this chapter we hope to give you a few guidelines.

First, it's important to understand how boys and girls differ in the way they are tempted sexually. Girls are attracted mainly by the *emotional* aspects of a relationship. They want security, a strong, handsome prince to sweep them into his arms and take care of them.

They are much more interested in someone who cares for them, knows what he believes and is open and friendly than in someone who displays himself in revealing clothing.

Boys are just the opposite. They can be sexually excited by the mere sight of a woman. If she has a low-cut dress, a revealing blouse or tight trousers, their imagination immediately begins to work overtime.

We can sum it up by saying that girls are attracted chiefly by *security* and strength of *character* while sexual temptation for a boy is based on *sight* and *imagination*.

That's why it's so important that girls, in particular, dress sensibly. Avoid low-cut fashions, dresses that are slit up the sides, very tight jeans and clothing that is really too small and, as a result, has the same revealing effect.

Boys, too, need to be careful how they dress. Don't go in for very tight trousers, wide studded belts or other clothing that is often used by homosexuals.

Confusing Dress

The Bible has quite a bit to say about clothing. It tells us of God's hatred for clothes that makes it difficult to tell whether you're a girl or a boy (see Deuteronomy 22 verse 5).

Some men try to get sexual satisfaction out of dressing in women's clothing, and women by dressing as men. This sinful practice is called *transvestism*. Some transvestites convince themselves that they should be the opposite sex to the one God made them. They then demand a *sex change* operation.

Although doctors can give drugs to make a man develop breasts and speak with a woman's voice, sex change operations are never fully successful. They simply aren't part of God's plan for men and women.

In Jude verse 23 we are urged to have a certain attitude to clothes

'stained' by sin. What should that attitude be? _____

_____ In other words, we should avoid clothing that might in any way be associated with sinful acts. That includes things that are usually worn by *prostitutes* (women who offer to have sex with men for money) or homosexuals, as well as very revealing clothes that are obviously intended to cause others to sin. Girls, if when you're older you go around without wearing a bra you might be following the latest trend — but you might also be causing extra unnecessary temptations to boys and men.

It's very likely that you know adults of your own sex (your parents, youth group leaders or even teachers) whom you look up to and admire. Think about the kind of clothing they wear. Is it deliberately revealing or intended to confuse their sexual identity? Probably not. Then follow their good example.

In Colossians 3:12 we are told to 'wear' certain things. Write them

down here._____

_____

_____

Then begin to learn how to wear them in all areas of your life.

Words like modesty, decorum and decency aren't very popular these days. Many people use clothes and the way they dress to show off their bodies in the wrong kind of way. We need to be aware of this and not follow this kind of attitude.

We aren't, of course, suggesting that you wear plain, old-fashioned clothes that will make you look ridiculous. You can find clothes that are smart without being sexually stimulating.

Can I Go Nude?

The Bible has a number of things to say about *nudity,* too.

At the beginning of creation, in the Garden of Eden, Adam and

Eve were naked but they weren't _____

(Genesis 2 verse 25). Then they sinned and, realising their nakedness, sewed fig leaves together to cover themselves (3 verse 7). Finally *God* provided them with clothing made from animal skins (3 verse 21).

After that, whenever the Bible mentions nudity outside of marriage, it is considered to be wrong. (See, for instance, Genesis 9 verses 20 to 23; Ezekiel 16 verses 36 to 39; and Revelation 3 verse 18.)

Of course, there's nothing wrong with very young brothers and sisters sharing the same bath, or with you undressing with others of your sex for sport or swimming. It's the *parading around* of nudity, particularly in front of those of the opposite sex, that is wrong.

Topless Bathing?

Some Christian young people today ask the question: 'Can I go topless, especially on beaches overseas?' The answer is yes — if you're a boy! If you're a girl and you go topless, you are without a doubt going to cause problems for boys and men.

Going topless might give you 'that liberated feeling' but, as long as the breasts remain the important part of sex that they are in western society, it is quite simply wrong.

Incidentally, we've heard of girls whose nipples have been very badly burnt by the sun — and they've decided never to be so 'liberated' again!

Many young people go abroad with their parents on holiday where there is topless and even nude bathing. How can you cope in such situations?

There is no simple answer. If you're a young man, you'll need to learn how to turn your eyes and control your thought life. (By the way, it might come as a surprise to know that full nudity causes fewer problems to most people than tantalising clothing. That's why striptease — undressing slowly and seductively — is so popular.)

Learn how you can have a great holiday without letting these things become a big problem to you. Don't go out of your way looking for topless bathers. That would be asking for trouble!

The Bible urges young men and women to 'avoid the passions of youth' (2 Timothy 2 verse 22). If you know that being around where topless bathing takes place isn't going to be a help to you, ask your parents if you can do something away from the beach or go to another beach. Far better that than face unnecessary temptations.

Pray for God to help you, share your concerns with a friend or parent and believe that you can have total victory. Take your thoughts captive and make them obedient to Christ (2 Corinthians 10 verse 5). If you do, we *know* you'll have a great holiday.

Back to Nature?

Some people believe that the innocence of the Garden of Eden can be restored through nudist colonies and so-called 'back to nature' activities.

First, as we've already seen, this is not what the Bible teaches. Second, right through puberty and adolescence you'll have enough adjustments to make and it's very unlikely that you would find nudism anything more than a big hindrance. Reject it!

Finally, learn to wear the right kind of things and, above all, remember that 'you are clothed, so to speak, with the life of Christ himself' (Galatians 3 verse 27).

Something to talk about

Have a look at a catalogue or teenage magazine with fashionable clothes in it. Are there ones there that you should avoid? If so, why?

15

Danger:
men that lurk

Right from when you were very small, you were almost certainly told not to talk to strangers or accept lifts or sweets from them. You might have wondered what sort of people these strangers were or what kind of things they might do to you.

Usually they aren't horrible monsters but people who've had a very unhappy upbringing and now give way to their own sinful desires. That doesn't mean that you should just feel sorry for them. They need to be sorted out — and if that means, among other things, going to prison or psychiatric hospital, then they must be sent there.

These people are usually men who give way to sexual temptations by abusing children. They might just show their sex organs to a child (*exhibitionism*) or play with the child's sex organs (*interfering* or *molesting)* or force a young girl to have full sex with them (*rape*).

In some cases, once these men have committed their sinful act, they feel so guilty about what they've done that, for some strange reason, they want to harm or even kill the child they've just abused.

Being Careful

At your age you need to be wise when it comes to going out on your own, especially if you're a girl. That doesn't mean that you need to be terrified and live constantly in fear. God *will* take care of you.

His angels are guarding you (Matthew 18 verse 10) and he promises to protect people (Proverbs 2 verse 8). Now write down Psalm 140 verse 1 and make it your prayer if you're worried about this kind of

thing. _____

_____

_____

_____

But it's still important to be wise and not get yourself into situations where you could easily be attacked. Find out the danger areas in your own district. They might be woods, large parks or inner city areas. Then, once you know them, keep away unless you're with someone else.

One of the saddest things about child sexual abuse is that in over half the cases the child is acquainted with the person who does it. It may be an adult friend of the family, a youth leader or even a close relative. (Sexual sin between family members who aren't married to each other, such as parents and children, or brothers and sisters, is known as *incest* and is always wrong.)

In such cases the child might not know what to do. Should he keep quiet about it? If he does talk to someone, will that person believe him? Will it mean automatically losing the person's friendship? Will the person who did it have to go prison? Will the child have to stand up in court and say what happened?

Supposing *you* were sexually abused by an adult. What would you do? Even if it hasn't happened to you, one day you may get to know someone who has been a victim, so it's important to think these things through.

Here are some guidelines:

1. Your body belongs to God

Remember that, if you're a Christian, your body has become

_____

_____

(1 Corinthians 6 verse 19). Your body now belongs to God. Always remember that no one at all has the right to touch it sexually until you are married. That is true, even if you aren't a Christian.

2. Don't pretend

If an adult has played with you sexually, admit to yourself that it happened. Don't pretend it was just an accident. Then, if possible, tell the person who did it that he mustn't do it again.

If he *does* try to do it again, say no to him in a firm way that really means business. He knows what he is doing, probably feels guilty about it and almost certainly will stop. Don't be afraid to run away from him if that's the only way to get him to stop.

3. Tell someone else

Don't be afraid to tell someone else if you've been sexually abused, even if you've been sworn to secrecy about it. That sort of secret won't help you or the person who abused you. Talk to your parents or — if for some reason that's not possible — a teacher or church leader. You could also phone Childline or your local council helpline for advice and guidance.

You may be a bit worried about doing that, especially if the person who abused you is someone you know and really like. But it's important that you do it because you need protection and he needs help.

If, by any chance, he's a Christian, he will need dealing with by the church leaders. He'll have to face up to his very serious sin, repent of it and come under the authority and discipline of the church leaders, as well as having to confess his crime to the police.

During that time, he probably won't be allowed to spend time with you — or with any other young people. But if he's a real friend, he'll be glad in the end you've told and broken your promise.

There are many, many people who were once child abusers and are now happily married and living as good Christians.

Jesus Christ provides help for even the worst sinners.

Another worry is that, if you tell someone about what's happened, you'll have to go to court and the person, if convicted, might end up in prison. Let's deal with the two problems separately.

First, fear of court shouldn't stop a person telling the truth. In more and more cases children are being allowed to give evidence on video or to the judge in private rather than having to stand up in court. If they're worried about this, they should talk about it well before they have to give evidence.

Second, there is the worry that a person who used to be nice in many ways might have to go to prison. Jesus once said about a person who causes children to sin: 'It would be better for him if a large millstone were tied round his neck and he were thown into the sea' (Luke 17 verse 2).

It might seem a hard thing to say, but prison might well be part of that person's healing.

If It Happens

You may have been abused sexually when you were younger. If you were, you may find you still feel bad deep down inside. You may lie awake at night worrying that it might happen again or be afraid of sex in marriage or not want to grow up sexually.

You may have nightmares or feel like murdering the person who did those things to you. You may even think about ending your own life.

If you're in that position, we have good news for you. Write down in your own words what Jesus said in John 8 verse 36.

_____

_____

He can set you free from all those horrible feelings you might have. He'll heal your mind and help you to be the kind of person you were intended to be.

Even if it happened a very long time ago, talk to someone about it, share your worries and fears and know the healing of the mind and memory that only Jesus can give.

He'll help you to remove any root of bitterness and hatred you might have (Hebrews 12 verse 15). And you might even learn to turn hatred into godly love for the person who did those things to you. You could then tell the person you forgive him. Wouldn't that be great?

If you're a Christian you are a child of God, a son of the King, one of his chosen people. Live like it. Be a success in all that you do. Don't allow the past to hold you back.

Something to talk about

What sort of advice would you give a friend who told you that he or she had been sexually abused by an adult? What would you suggest he or she does if the adult tries it again?

16

Falling in love

It all started on the sofa after the party. Fourteen-year-old John and his 13-year-old girlfriend, Fran, had enjoyed the evening, especially spending time with all their friends from church.

The party had finished a bit earlier than anyone had expected and when they got to John's house they found that his parents were still not back from *their* evening out.

Suddenly, they were completely on their own together. Both had already decided in their minds that one day they wanted to try out some of the things they'd heard about in the school playground from their friends. Now was their chance.

First there was the kissing. It was a deep kind — like the sort you see on films — far more exciting than giving your mum a quick peck on the cheek at night.

Then their hands started exploring each other's bodies. First, they tried to pretend to themselves and to each other that the touches were just accidental. Then, as they got a bit more daring, they kept trying to stop because they knew that what they were beginning to do was wrong.

Soon, though, they managed to ignore God's voice to their hearts as the sexual excitement grew. Their hands were now touching each other just where they wanted to. The desire to go further and further was now so great that their bodies were actually shaking as if they were shivering in the cold.

Just then they heard the key in the door. John's parents were home! Quickly they straightened out their clothes and hair and moved apart slightly. A moment later they said a quick goodnight as John's dad took Fran home. They left each other feeling very guilty, frustrated and highly disappointed.

The following day when they met before the church meeting, both immediately had that same feeling of excitement and frustration, mixed with deep guilt, that they had had the previous night. They wanted to start all over again — this time going much, much further . . . .

More Than a Feeling

Let's be very honest with you. You could easily end up in the same kind of wrong situation if you are not very careful, especially when you start going out regularly with someone of the opposite sex.

In this chapter we'll be looking at the question: 'What is love?' We'll also be giving you some standards for when *you* fall in love and start going out with someone.

So what is love? Pop songs tell us that love is just *sex*, as we've already mentioned. Then there are other people who say that love is merely a *feeling*. You're walking down the road one day and suddenly you see someone of the opposite sex and fall head over heels in love with him or her. There's nothing you can do about it — you're hooked!

The truth is that love is much more than either of these extremes. Love is also *respect, trust, giving* and *commitment*. You may like someone and even feel sexually excited by them. But you can't love them fully until you get to know them and are committed to them through the bad times as well as the good.

Some people talk about love at first sight. Well, that's just impossible. You can't truly love someone when you don't know their name or anything about them. James Dobson describes such 'falling in love with love' as *temporary* and *self-centred*.

Real love, on the other hand, involves learning how to get on with each other in a committed relationship until one or other of the partners dies. People in love who are married can and will, of course, have differences of opinion but they are willing and ready to put the other first and to listen to his or her opinions.

Going Out Together

There's a lot of pressure on young people to go out with each other. Some go out simply because it's the thing that everyone else does. Yet the truth is that some teenagers are just not interested in going out at the moment because they're too busy with studying, sport or hobbies.

If you're not the type for having a boyfriend or girlfriend, don't worry. There's certainly nothing wrong with you! Both of us went through our teen years without going out much.

If, on the other hand, you *are* interested in going out with those of the opposite sex, here are some important guidelines:

1. Don't be 'unequally yoked'

The Bible says very clearly that it is wrong for a Christian to marry a non-Christian. Look up 2 Corinthians 6 verses 14 to 15 and write it down here._____

_____

_____

_____

_____

This applies, not only to marriage, but to going out together. There's no point in forming such a relationship with someone outside of Christ.

Do you know the best way to help someone out of a river when he's fallen in? If you hold out your hand to him and he grabs you, he can easily pull you in. But if you hold a tree branch out for him to grab on to, then you're able to let go if he begins to drag you in.

Being unequally yoked with someone could easily result in you being pulled into his or her wrong ways. Let go before it's too late!

2. Don't spend too much time on your own together

Learn to enjoy the person's friendship in company with others of your own age, especially young people from your local church. Don't spend lots of time on your own together in places where it would be easy for you to fall into sexual sin.

3. Set your standards

Decide before you start that you won't play with sin in the area of sex. Determine that you'll break the relationship if things ever start to get out of hand.

It is wrong for an unmarried boy and girl deliberately to stir each other up sexually.

That means avoiding *deep kissing* (also known as *French kissing),* touching or playing with each other's sex organs (*petting)* or bringing each other to a climax (*heavy petting).* All these things are an important part of preparation for sex (*foreplay)* and should be saved for marriage. Using the mouth to stimulate the sex organs (*oral sex)* is equally wrong — and can cause the spread of a number of sexually transmitted diseases.

Getting It Right

4. Be ready to learn

Going out with someone of the opposite sex can be good training for life in general. Learn to appreciate the person as a human being made in God's image rather than a sex object. Boys have a great opportunity to find out how girls think and girls will begin to know the sort of thing boys are interested in.

It can be great fun learning!

5. Discover the differences

We've already discussed the fact that boys and girls are different in more than just their bodies. Girls tend to look for 'love' in a relationship while boys want to be respected and admired.

Boys also tend to be more interested in the body rather than the person whereas girls usually have a more balanced approach!

Get to know these differences. It will be a great help later on when you are going out with a possible future marriage partner.

6. Lust isn't love

Don't forget that sexual desire isn't love. If you give way just a little to sexual desires you are asking for big problems. The temptation to sin further — even going 'all the way' — will then be much greater.

Everyone has sexual desires and temptations. Don't give way to them. Control your sexual desires — don't let them control *you*.

A Future Partner

When you're older, you will almost certainly have a deep desire to get married. No doubt, like most other people, you'll start looking for a future partner.

Always remember that God will guide you to your future marriage partner when the time is right — though he certainly won't just place someone in your lap! The Bible says to young men: 'Find a wife and you find a good thing; it shows that the Lord is good to you' (Proverbs 18 verse 22). Don't just pray for a wife — go and look for one!

Supposing you're older and you meet the partner of your dream. You get to know each other and then you decide to get married. How long should you wait?

It's a fact that rushed marriages often lead to disaster. You need to get to know a possible future partner very well before you decide to 'take the plunge' into marriage.

Find out how he or she thinks and reacts in different situations. Do you have very strong differences or do you agree on most (though not necessarily all) things? Does the other person speak highly about you or treat you like nothing?

First learn how you get on together. Then you'll know how good the marriage will be. Don't be ruled by your emotions. Use your head as well as your heart!

It's far better to stay single for the rest of your life than to get married to someone because you're desperate for a partner. Read Proverbs 21 verse 19 and 25 verse 24 to see what we mean!

Make sure you're good friends, too. Do you share similar hobbies and interests? Are you good friends as well as in love with each other? These will be very important things to think about when the time comes.

Above all, the best relationship has Jesus Christ as the third person in it. If you are both Christians, make sure that you pray together and that you feel comfortable about talking over the things that mean so much to you as Christians. If the spiritual side isn't right in a Christian marriage, then the relationship isn't either.

Getting Engaged

Let's imagine that you've found someone who you get on well with and want to marry. The two of you become *engaged*, in other words agree to get married, and the man then gives the woman an engagement ring.

As the great day of your wedding gets nearer, and you grow closer and closer, you'll almost certainly find the sexual temptations getting bigger. How do you cope then?

Always remember that sexual 'practice' for marriage is a total lie of the devil, as we've already seen. The only right kind of practice begins on your wedding night with a clear conscience before God and other people.

A few weeks before your wedding you will probably want to read a good book on the techniques of sex in marriage. But until then you have no business to read up on techniques or all the other details needed for a happy sexual life in marriage. Reading such things now will only cause you more problems and temptations, with years to wait to try them out.

In Colossians 3:5 we read about a number of things that we should put to death. Write them down here. _____

_____

_____

Now begin to do just that with your own thoughts, words and deeds.

Finally, be prayerful about that relationship. Don't let it develop further unless you believe it to be right. And don't be afraid to stop it if things don't work out.

May you know God's wisdom in this important area of your life.

Something to talk about

Read again the first few paragraphs of this chapter about John and Fran. Now see if you can point out where they went wrong and how they could avoid sinning.

17

Standing for truth

Despite all their boasting about their sexual abilities, many teenagers today are almost clueless about the facts of life.

Eight out of ten teenagers have had no sex education at home, while at school, sex education often fails to provide answers to some of the most important questions.

Some of the things people even older than you believe about sex would be funny if they weren't so sad. Some girls think that the Pill should be inserted into the vagina!

Some boys think 'lesbian' means 'prostitute', while we heard of one who even thought that venereal disease (STD — sexually transmitted disease) could be caught from a rare butterfly from Africa!

Most serious of all is the widely-held wrong belief among girls that they can't get pregnant the first time they have sex because their hymen hasn't been broken (see page 59).

A Privilege

All this means that, having read so far, you're in a very privileged position. You probably know a lot more about sex than many of your friends. Over the years as you go through your teens you'll be able to refer back to parts of this book to help you remember different things as you need them.

You've found out the facts of life in a straightforward, honest way so that you won't be left in any doubt.

If you've read the message for parents at the beginning of this book, you'll know about the game using sperm and egg tokens to try to get some children to talk about sex. Is it any wonder that some young people are so mixed up and find it difficult to talk to their parents?!

Other children get even more confused. Groups from schools in the London area were taken to a theatre where they saw a play in support of lesbians. The stage had a backcloth of giant Pill packets, a Cindy house made from sanitary towels and a toy poodle made out of blown-up contraceptives! One of the songs in the play was, sadly: 'I got the curse' (an expression sometimes used to describe periods).

Can you imagine how confused the children must have been? We hope you're grateful to God that you got a proper understanding of sex before you had some of these strange ideas thrown at you.

Taking a Stand

As a young person in such a privileged position, you can stand up for truth in the area of sex at school and among your friends. We're not suggesting that you show off your knowledge, but when you hear people at school pretending they know about aspects of sex or are totally confused, you can tell them the truth.

When they start saying that sex outside of marriage is OK, you can now give them a number of good reasons why it's wrong.

It won't take you by surprise anymore when you start hearing them talk about goings-on in the bike sheds, masturbation in the toilets or boys and girls touching each others' bodies (*petting*) in the playground. You'll be able to take your stand for truth, telling people what you know to be right and wrong.

Don't worry if you're not sure what to say or how to say it. Jesus said that, when Christians stand before others in such a way, they will be given the right words to speak (Matthew 10 verse 19). According to verse 20, who will give them those words _____ ?

Should I Opt Out?

It's the same when your school has lessons on sex education. It's just possible that your parents will be given the choice of allowing you to go or not — and they'll almost certainly ask what you think.

You might want to opt out because you're worried about being influenced by unhelpful attitudes or wrong teaching.

Our advice to you is that, even if you do have a choice, you should go along to these classes and be ready to speak up for biblical standards. It may be the only time in their lives that the young people attending will hear God's attitude to sex and morality — from you!

Look up 1 Timothy 4 verse 12 and write it down here. _____

_____

_____

Be brave — and God *will* help you.

Something to talk about

What are the areas where you will find it most difficult to stand up for truth in the area of sex? How do you think God (through his Holy Spirit) will help you?

18

Pressing on

Now that you've read most of this book, you may be wondering how you can possibly make it through the next 10 or 20 years before you get married!

Source of Strength

We believe you can, especially if you belong to Jesus and are being filled constantly with the Holy Spirit. A Christian has the greatest source of power anyone could possibly have. That doesn't mean that you won't have sexual temptatons. Far from it. But you'll have God's power on your side ready to give you strength, especially when you're at your weakest.

Sexual temptations are perhaps the strongest temptations there are, as we've already seen. When you're in the middle of them, you'll hardly be able to think of anything else.

Satan's Lies

At that time Satan will start putting in your mind ideas like:
'Live for now.'
'It won't matter if you find out what sex is like — just this once.'
'You can't manage to wait all that time until you're married.'
'No one will know.'

These are all total lies, of course. Yet so many young people — and older ones, too — are foolishly listening to Satan's voice and suffering for years as a result.

Here are two of the most common things people say about sexual temptations. Look up 1 Corinthians 10 verse 13 and write under each excuse what God says about it:

1. 'I must be the only one in the world to have that kind of temptation.'

_____

_____

2. 'If I have sexual temptations any stronger than that, I might not be able to resist.'

_____

_____

_____

Way of Escape

Escaping from temptation sometimes means taking drastic action. As a young man, Joseph knew that he might sin if he stayed around. What did he do (Genesis 39 verses 11 to 13)? _____

_____ Doing that is a sign of strength, not weakness.

Instead of listening to people around you, listen to God's voice. He tells you to put on the whole armour of God so that you

can _____

_____

_____ (Ephesians 6 verse 11).

Once you have put your armour on, keep it on and don't give up in the battle like the sons of Ephraim did (Psalm 78 verses 9 to 11). God is able to keep you from falling and help you stand before God (Jude verse 4).

At some time over the next few years you'll probably have a chance to commit sexual sin. The opportunity may come very suddenly and seem so easy to give in to.

Recognise that it will almost certainly happen to you. Then decide right now that you're going to live a pure life.

You were made to succeed. Believe that you're going to live free from sexual sin in a world that's increasingly impure. Look forward to enjoying sex in marriage.

Accept the challenge of living for Jesus Christ. And with God's help we know you'll be a success.

Something to talk about

Look up Ephesians 6 verses 10 to 18 again and talk about what each
piece of armour means. (For more on the armour of God and how
to be a good soldier of Jesus, read Arthur Wallis's superb book for
young people, *Into Battle* [Kingsway].).

Some questions about sex

Here are a few questions for you to work through to test yourself on the contents of this book. It's not an examination but a way of helping you to see how much you've understood about sex from this book.

If you aren't sure of an answer, please leave a blank space. Use drawings if you want to, and if you think they will help.

1. Who invented sex? _____

2. There are two reasons why sex was invented. What are they?

_____

_____

3. Does God think that sex in marriage is something good or bad?
_____ Why? _____

_____

_____

4. What are these parts of a boy's body for?

a. Penis (two reasons) _____

_____

b. Testicles_____

_____

c. Urethra (two reasons) _____

_____

5. What is an erection of the penis and what is it for? _____

_____

_____

6. Is it wrong to have an erection? _____ When a boy has one, what's the best thing to do? _____

_____

7. What is a nocturnal emission? _____

_____

Is it something good or bad? _____ Why? _____

_____

8. What are sperm cells for? _____

_____

9. What are these parts of a girl's body for?

a. Vagina _____

_____

b. Urethra _____

_____

c. Clitoris _____

_____

d. Breasts _____

_____

e. Uterus _____

_____

f. Ovaries _____

_____

10. What is a period? _____

_____

How is the blood kept from getting on the girl's clothes? _____

_____

11. What is fertilisation of the egg and sperm? _____

_____

What happens next? _____

_____

12. Describe sex between a husband and wife in marriage. _____

_____

_____

_____

_____

_____

_____

13. What is contraception?_____

_____

14. Does God say that sex outside of marriage is right or wrong?
_____ Why?_____

_____

_____

15. People who commit sexual sin often have to suffer the results.
Explain what could happen in these areas:

a. Having a baby or having an abortion _____

_____

b. Sexually transmitted diseases (STD) _____

_____

c. Being 'secondhand' _____

_____

d. Being ashamed _____

_____

16. What changes should a boy look for in his body as he reaches puberty? _____

_____

_____

_____

_____

_____

17. What changes should a girl look for in her body as she reaches puberty? _____

_____

_____

_____

_____

_____

18. What is masturbation? _____

_____

19. Is it a sexual sin of the kind the Bible talks about, or just an ordinary sin? _____

_____

20. What should you say to God if you masturbate?_____

21. How strong are sexual temptations? _____

22. Why is it wrong to look at sexy pictures and videos? _____

_____

_____

Why is it a bit like taking drugs? _____

_____

23. What is the best thing to do if you are tempted to have sex with someone? _____

_____

24. Is it good or bad to run from sexual temptation?_____

25. Why should you wait until marriage before having sex? ____

_____

Can God help you to stay pure? _____

26. Why is homosexual sin wrong? _____

_____

_____

27. If two boys or two girls 'play around' with each other's bodies — just once — does that mean that they are homosexuals? _____ Why? _____

_____

28. Now write down a prayer to God asking him to help you wait until you're married before you have sex. Tell him that you're looking forward to having sex with your future partner after you get married.

_____

_____

_____

_____

_____

_____

Some words and their meaning

abortion — killing of a baby in his or her mother's uterus (womb) before birth

adolescent — a young man or woman whose body has grown up sexually but who is not yet an adult

AIDS (acquired immune deficiency syndrome) — a killer disease, widespread among homosexuals and, increasingly, heterosexuals, caught mainly by sexual contact but also, occasionally, through infected blood transfusions (blood is now checked to prevent this happening) and using dirty needles to inject drugs

bisexual — a person who has sexual attraction towards those of the opposite sex but who also wants to commit homosexual or lesbian sin

circumcision — a small operation to remove the flap of skin (the prepuce, or foreskin) covering the end of a boy's penis

climax (see 'orgasm')

clitoris — a small sensitive rod-shaped organ, containing erectile tissue, located under the skin in a girl's pubic region

contraceptive — a device to enable a husband and wife to enjoy sex without having a baby every year or so

ejaculation — the climax of sex for a husband when semen is spurted out of the end of his penis into his wife's vagina; also when semen is spurted out of a boy's penis as a nocturnal emission or spontaneous ejaculation or as a result of masturbation

erection — when the penis of a boy becomes hard and stiff, sticking up at an angle of about 45°; also when the clitoris of a girl becomes hard and stiff under the skin of the vulva region

exhibitionism — sexual desire by a man to show his sex organs to others, especially women and girls

Fallopian tube — the funnel-shaped tube in a woman where the egg (ovum) of the wife is fertilised by sperm from the husband

fertilisation — the point when a male sperm cell joins together with a female egg (ovum) to begin forming a new baby

'gay' (see 'homosexual')

group sex — sexual sin involving three or more people

heterosexual — a person who has normal sexual attractions to people of the opposite sex

homosexual — a man who desires to commit sexual sin with other men or boys

hymen — a membrane that partly covers the entrance to the vagina of an unmarried girl or woman

incest — sexual sin between members of the same family who are not married to each other (such as brothers and sisters or parents and children)

intercourse (see 'sexual intercourse')

lesbian — a woman who desires to commit sexual sin with other women

masturbation — playing with one's own sexual organs to produce a pleasant feeling, often resulting in an orgasm

menopause — the stage when a woman (usually aged between 40 and 50) stops producing ova (eggs) from her ovaries and can no longer have children

mutual masturbation — sexual sin in which two people of the same sex play with each other's sex organs

nocturnal emission — the removal of surplus sperm from a boy's body while he is asleep, sometimes accompanied by a sexual dream

orgasm — climax of the sex act when sperm is ejaculated from the husband's penis or when the wife reaches the height of her sexual enjoyment; also the end result of masturbation, a nocturnal emission or a spontaneous ejaculation

ovaries — two organs in a girl's body that produce an ovum (egg) each month which then passes along the Fallopian tube

penis — the fleshy tube-like organ between a boy's legs that is used for both passing urine and, in marriage, for sex

petting — sexual sin in which a boy and girl play with each other's sex organs

pornography — videos, films, books and magazines with pictures or words that are designed to stir people up sexually

pregnancy — the stage when a wife is carrying a developing baby (foetus) in her uterus (womb)

prostitute — a woman who sells her body for sexual sin

puberty — the stage when a young person's body begins to grow up sexually

rape — forced sex, usually by a man

semen — white, cloudy, sticky fluid containing sperm cells that spurts out of the erect penis of an adolescent boy or a man

sexual intercourse — the sex act between a husband and wife

sodomy — sexual sin, usually among homosexuals, in which the anus (back passage) is used as a pretend vagina

sperm cell — a tiny cell with a tail, formed in the husband's testicle, that swims to the Fallopian tubes of the wife to join with the egg and form a new baby

spontaneous ejaculation — a rare occurrence when sperm spurts out of a boy's penis, for no apparent reason, while he is concentrating on something else

STD (sexually transmitted diseases) — diseases, usually of the sex organs, which can only be spread through sexual sin (sometimes still called VD — venereal diseases)

sterilisation — an operation to prevent a woman from having any more children

testicles — two small organs that hang in a special bag of skin (the scrotum) between a boy's legs and which produce sperm cells

transvestite — a man who gets sexual satisfaction out of wearing women's clothes (or a woman wearing man's clothes)

uterus — the part of a girl's sexual equipment where a baby will grow

vagina — the main sex organ of the girl, in which, when she is married, the husband's penis is inserted during sex and through which their baby is born

vasectomy — an operation on a husband to prevent sperm passing into the penis and fertilising eggs in his wife's body

venereal diseases (VD) — (see 'STD')

virgin — a boy or girl, man or woman, who has never engaged in sexual intercourse

womb (see 'uterus')

Index

Notes